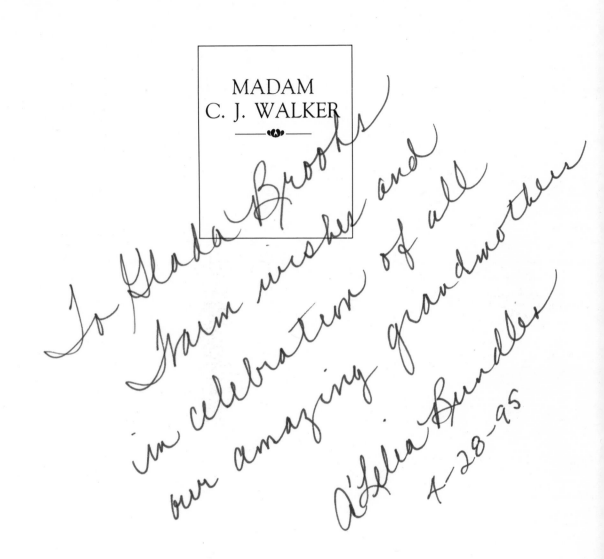

MADAM
C. J. WALKER

To Glada Brooks
warm wishes and
in celebration of all
our amazing grandmothers

A'Lelia Bundles
4-28-95

MADAM
C. J. WALKER

A'Lelia Perry Bundles

Senior Consulting Editor
Nathan Irvin Huggins
Director
W.E.B. Du Bois Institute for Afro-American Research
Harvard University

CHELSEA HOUSE PUBLISHERS
New York   Philadelphia

Chelsea House Publishers

Editor-in-Chief   Remmel Nunn
Managing Editor   Karyn Gullen Browne
Copy Chief   Juliann Barbato
Picture Editor   Adrian G. Allen
Art Director   Maria Epes
Deputy Copy Chief   Mark Rifkin
Assistant Art Director   Noreen Romano
Manufacturing Manager   Gerald Levine
Systems Manager   Lindsey Ottman
Production Manager   Joseph Romano
Production Coordinator   Marie Claire Cebrián

Black Americans of Achievement

Senior Editor   Richard Rennert

Staff for   MADAM C. J. WALKER

Text Editor   Marian W. Taylor
Copy Editor   Brian Sookram
Editorial Assistant   Michele Haddad
Picture Researcher   Wendy P. Wills
Designer   Ghila Krajzman
Cover Illustration   Janet Hamlin, from a photograph of Madam C. J. Walker
from the Walker Collection of A'Lelia Bundles.

3 5 7 9 8 6 4

Library of Congress Cataloging-in-Publication Data

Bundles, A'Lelia.
    Madam C. J. Walker, entrepreneur/by A'Lelia Bundles.
        p.   cm.—(Black Americans of achievement)
    Includes bibliographical references.
    Summary: A biography of the Afro-American businesswoman
whose invention of facial creams and other cosmetics led to great
financial success and who, throughout her life, devoted herself to
many social and political causes.
    ISBN 1-55546-615-X
        0-7910-0251-9 (pbk.)
    1. Walker, C. J., Madam, 1867–1919. 2. Afro-American
women   executives—Biography. 3. Cosmetics   industry—United
States—History. [1. Walker, C. J., Madam, 1867–1919. 2. Afro-
Americans—Biography. 3. Cosmetics industry—History.] I. Title.
II. Series.
HD9970.5.C672W353
338.7′66855′092—dc20   89-77285
[B]   CIP
[92]   AC

Frontispiece: *Madam C. J. Walker, America's first black female millionaire, established her company headquarters in this Indianapolis, Indiana, building in 1912.*

CONTENTS

BLACK AMERICANS OF ACHIEVEMENT

RALPH ABERNATHY
civil rights leader

MUHAMMAD ALI
heavyweight champion

RICHARD ALLEN
religious leader and social activist

LOUIS ARMSTRONG
musician

ARTHUR ASHE
tennis great

JOSEPHINE BAKER
entertainer

JAMES BALDWIN
author

BENJAMIN BANNEKER
scientist and mathematician

AMIRI BARAKA
poet and playwright

COUNT BASIE
bandleader and composer

ROMARE BEARDEN
artist

JAMES BECKWOURTH
frontiersman

MARY MCLEOD
BETHUNE
educator

BLANCHE BRUCE
politician

RALPH BUNCHE
diplomat

GEORGE WASHINGTON
CARVER
botanist

CHARLES CHESNUTT
author

BILL COSBY
entertainer

PAUL CUFFE
merchant and abolitionist

FATHER DIVINE
religious leader

FREDERICK DOUGLASS
abolitionist editor

CHARLES DREW
physician

W.E.B. DU BOIS
scholar and activist

PAUL LAURENCE DUNBAR
poet

KATHERINE DUNHAM
dancer and choreographer

MARIAN WRIGHT EDELMAN
civil rights leader and lawyer

DUKE ELLINGTON
bandleader and composer

RALPH ELLISON
author

JULIUS ERVING
basketball great

JAMES FARMER
civil rights leader

ELLA FITZGERALD
singer

MARCUS GARVEY
black-nationalist leader

DIZZY GILLESPIE
musician

PRINCE HALL
social reformer

W. C. HANDY
father of the blues

WILLIAM HASTIE
educator and politician

MATTHEW HENSON
explorer

CHESTER HIMES
author

BILLIE HOLIDAY
singer

JOHN HOPE
educator

LENA HORNE
entertainer

LANGSTON HUGHES
poet

ZORA NEALE HURSTON
author

JESSE JACKSON
civil rights leader and politician

JACK JOHNSON
heavyweight champion

JAMES WELDON JOHNSON
author

SCOTT JOPLIN
composer

BARBARA JORDAN
politician

MARTIN LUTHER KING, JR.
civil rights leader

ALAIN LOCKE
scholar and educator

JOE LOUIS
heavyweight champion

RONALD MCNAIR
astronaut

MALCOLM X
militant black leader

THURGOOD MARSHALL
Supreme Court justice

ELIJAH MUHAMMAD
religious leader

JESSE OWENS
champion athlete

CHARLIE PARKER
musician

GORDON PARKS
photographer

SIDNEY POITIER
actor

ADAM CLAYTON POWELL, JR.
political leader

LEONTYNE PRICE
opera singer

A. PHILIP RANDOLPH
labor leader

PAUL ROBESON
singer and actor

JACKIE ROBINSON
baseball great

BILL RUSSELL
basketball great

JOHN RUSSWURM
publisher

SOJOURNER TRUTH
antislavery activist

HARRIET TUBMAN
antislavery activist

NAT TURNER
slave revolt leader

DENMARK VESEY
slave revolt leader

MADAM C. J. WALKER
entrepreneur

BOOKER T. WASHINGTON
educator

HAROLD WASHINGTON
politician

WALTER WHITE
civil rights leader and author

RICHARD WRIGHT
author

ON
ACHIEVEMENT

——— ❧ ———

Coretta Scott King

Before you begin this book, I hope you will ask yourself what the word excellence means to you. I think that it's a question we should all ask, and keep asking as we grow older and change. Because the truest answer to it should never change. When you think of excellence, perhaps you think of success at work; or of becoming wealthy; or meeting the right person, getting married, and having a good family life.

Those important goals are worth striving for, but there is a better way to look at excellence. As Martin Luther King, Jr., said in one of his last sermons, "I want you to be first in love. I want you to be first in moral excellence. I want you to be first in generosity. If you want to be important, wonderful. If you want to be great, wonderful. But recognize that he who is greatest among you shall be your servant."

My husband, Martin Luther King, Jr., knew that the true meaning of achievement is service. When I met him, in 1952, he was already ordained as a Baptist preacher and was working towards a doctoral degree at Boston University. I was studying at the New England Conservatory and dreamed of accomplishments in music. We married a year later, and after I graduated the following year we moved to Montgomery, Alabama. We didn't know it then, but our notions of achievement were about to undergo a dramatic change.

You may have read or heard about what happened next. What began with the boycott of a local bus line grew into a national movement, and by the time he was assassinated in 1968 my husband had fashioned a black movement powerful enough to shatter forever the practice of racial segregation. What you may not have read about is where he got his method for resisting injustice without compromising his religious beliefs.

He adopted the strategy of nonviolence from a man of a different race, who lived in a distant country, and even practiced a different religion. The man was Mahatma Gandhi, the great leader of India, who devoted his life to serving humanity in the spirit of love and nonviolence. It was in these principles that Martin discovered his method for social reform. More than anything else, those two principles were the key to his achievements.

This book is about black Americans who served society through the excellence of their achievements. It forms a part of the rich history of black men and women in America—a history of stunning accomplishments in every field of human endeavor, from literature and art to science, industry, education, diplomacy, athletics, jurisprudence, even polar exploration.

Not all of the people in this history had the same ideals, but I think you will find something that all of them have in common. Like Martin Luther King, Jr., they all decided to become "drum majors" and serve humanity. In that principle—whether it was expressed in books, inventions, or song—they found something outside themselves to use as a goal and a guide. Something that showed them a way to serve others, instead of living only for themselves.

Reading the stories of these courageous men and women not only helps us discover the principles that we will use to guide our own lives but also teaches us about our black heritage and about America itself. It is crucial for us to know the heroes and heroines of our history and to realize that the price we paid in our struggle for equality in America was dear. But we must also understand that we have gotten as far as we have partly because America's democratic system and ideals made it possible.

We are still struggling with racism and prejudice. But the great men and women in this series are a tribute to the spirit of our democratic ideals and the system in which they have flourished. And that makes their stories special and worth knowing. ❧

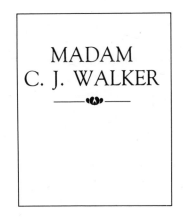

MADAM
C. J. WALKER

1

"MY OWN FACTORY ON MY OWN GROUND"

STATELY AND HANDSOME, 44-year-old Madam C. J. Walker was brimming with self-confidence as she arrived in Chicago for the 1912 convention of the National Negro Business League (NNBL). She was sure that she could persuade Booker T. Washington, the nation's most influential black spokesman and the NNBL president, to let her address the more than 200 black American entrepreneurs who had journeyed to this Illinois city. Washington had treated her cordially earlier in the year, when she visited Tuskegee Institute, the black vocational school he founded. Moreover, he was aware of Walker's fund-raising efforts for black education.

Poor for most of her life, Walker had invented a new hair-care product when she was 37. By the time she attended the Chicago convention seven years later, she owned and operated her own thriving business, the Madam C. J. Walker Manufacturing Company of Indianapolis, Indiana. Knowing it would encourage them, Walker wanted to tell other black women about her work. Meanwhile, she paid careful attention to the men who addressed the daily sessions.

Born to former slaves on a Louisiana cotton plantation, Sarah Breedlove Walker spent 20 years as a laundress. At the age of 37, however, she invented a hair-care product that made her the wealthiest black woman in the United States.

11

At the convention's opening meeting, Walker listened closely to one success story after another. Massachusetts real estate broker Watt Terry, for example, told the audience how he had started his career by purchasing a single house; after selling it at a profit, he invested his money and eventually acquired 50 houses and 2 apartment buildings altogether worth half a million dollars.

The accounts of Terry and his fellow businessmen would have been striking under any circumstances. What made them truly remarkable, however, was the race of the speakers. Half a century earlier, almost all the blacks in America had been slaves. In 1860, one of every seven Americans was the property of another.

A handful of owners taught their slaves to read and write and encouraged them to learn skilled trades, but most slaveholders preferred to keep blacks illiterate. Teaching a slave to read, in fact, was a crime in many southern states, and several states passed laws prohibiting blacks from holding jobs that required literacy.

Thus, when the Civil War—and slavery—ended in 1865, blacks were ill equipped to enter the economic mainstream. Those who tried to start their own businesses found it almost impossible to borrow money from white bankers, and blacks who did manage to offer products or services found few white customers. Nevertheless, a number of enterprising blacks established such small but profitable operations as barbershops, catering firms, sail-making shops, funeral homes, pharmacies, and dry-goods stores.

By 1900, when Booker T. Washington, himself a former slave, founded the National Negro Business League to help promote black commerce, the United States boasted some 20,000 black-owned businesses. By the time of the 1912 convention, that number had doubled. But despite these impressive figures, most black Americans still lived in poverty. A black businessman was rare, a black business*woman* even rarer.

Walker found herself especially intrigued by the words of Anthony Overton, who described his Overton-Hygienic Manufacturing Company of Chicago as "the largest Negro manufacturing enterprise in the United States." From the sale of its products, which included cosmetics and baking powder, the Illinois firm had earned more than $117,000 during the previous year. This was just the kind of success Walker hoped to achieve with her own company.

When Overton finished speaking, Washington asked for questions from the audience. George Knox, publisher of the black Indianapolis newspaper *The Freeman*, stood up. "I arise to ask this convention for a few minutes of its time to hear a remarkable woman," he said. "She is Madam Walker, the manufacturer of hair goods and preparations."

Acting as though Knox had not spoken, Washington recognized another audience member. The frustrated Walker suspected that he looked down on her line of work: the manufacture and sale of hair treatments for blacks. Nevertheless, she resolved that the convention would hear from her, even if she had to commandeer the podium. At the next morning's session, she sat patiently through a long lecture by an Indianapolis banker, then another by a Texas banker. As each man returned to his seat, she tried to catch Washington's eye, but with no success.

Finally, while the audience was applauding Washington's remarks about the Texas banker, Walker sprang to her feet. "Surely you are not going to shut the door in my face," she said firmly. "I feel that I am in a business that is a credit to the womanhood of our race. I started in business seven years ago with only $1.50."

The audience looked at her with curiosity. Who was this determined woman with the satiny, cocoa-colored skin and the beautifully groomed hair?

Educator Booker T. Washington, the foremost black spokesman of the early 20th century, founded the National Negro Business League (NNBL) in 1900. Skeptical at first about female entrepreneurs, he ignored Walker at the 1912 NNBL convention, but he later hailed her as "one of the most progressive and successful businesswomen of our race."

"I am a woman who came from the cotton fields of the South," said Walker. "I was promoted from there to the washtub." This line drew a laugh: The position of washerwomen was hardly enviable. "Then I was promoted to the cook kitchen, and from there *I promoted myself* into the business of manufacturing hair goods and preparations," continued Walker in a strong voice. "I have built my own factory on my own ground." Now, serious attention replaced the audience's laughter.

"My object in life is not simply to make money for myself or to spend it on myself," Walker said. "I love to use a part of what I make in trying to help others."

Walker finished her speech and returned to her seat in a wave of applause. When it finally subsided, Knox took the floor. "I arise to attest all that this good woman has said concerning her business," he declared.

That evening, Walker's unscheduled speech was the talk of the convention. Delegates clustered around her after dinner, eager to learn more about this newcomer with the expensive clothes, dignified manner, and firm convictions.

Responding to her colleagues' questions, Walker said she believed that more black women should strike out on their own. "The girls and women of our race," she asserted, "must not be afraid to take hold of business endeavor and . . . wring success out of a number of business opportunities that lie at their very doors."

A few of the men disagreed; their wives, they said, should stay at home and take care of their families. But whether a woman should work or not was not the issue: Most black American women had no choice. Those who were unmarried, widowed, or single parents had to support themselves, and many of the married women had to augment the small incomes their husbands were able to earn.

Black women earned less than any other working group in America. Although a small number had managed to become schoolteachers or nurses, and a few had opened beauty parlors or seamstress shops, most rural black women worked on farms, and most of those in the cities took jobs—when they could find them—as maids, cooks, or laundresses. In the first decade of the 20th century, very few black women earned more than $1.50 per week. (At this point, the average unskilled white worker earned about $11 weekly.)

Walker told the conference delegates about the way her program helped black women. After learning the Walker System of hair care, either at one of her schools or through a correspondence course, a Walker agent could set up shop in her own home, receiving customers and selling Walker products. Her agents, said Walker, enjoyed both newfound independence and an increased income, allowing them to buy homes and send their children to school.

By 1912, Walker had trained more than 1,000 women. They were, she told her listeners, making $5, $10, and even $15 per day. "I have made it possible," she said proudly, "for many colored women

A trio of grocers proudly survey their immaculate shop. Only a generation away from slavery, some 40,000 enterprising black Americans had started their own businesses by 1912.

Friends of Indianapolis's new black YMCA assemble on its steps in 1913. In the front row are (from left) Freeman *publisher George Knox, Madam C. J. Walker, Booker T. Washington,* Indianapolis World *publisher Alex Manning, and YMCA executives R. W. Bullock and Thomas Taylor. Standing at the rear are Walker's longtime business associate, F. B. Ransom (left), and her physician, Colonel Joseph Ward.*

to abandon the washtub for more pleasant and profitable occupation."

As the Chicago convention ended, delegates continued to talk about Madam Walker and her unusual business practices. Even Washington, who had taken no official notice of her, would soon prove he had been impressed by this dynamic, highly motivated woman.

Several months later, Washington and other nationally known black leaders attended the dedication of the new black YMCA in Indianapolis. Sharing the stage with keynote speaker Washington were a number of prominent local blacks—including Madam C. J. Walker. The cosmetics manufacturer had stunned YMCA building-fund officials by contributing $1,000, the largest sum donated by any black benefactor.

Washington told the dedication ceremony's 1,200 guests that the new YMCA would improve the lives of the city's young men. "This building," he said, "should mean less crime, less drink, less gambling, less association with bad characters," and should make its users "more industrious, more ambitious, more economical." Walker must have been warmed when, at the end of his speech, Washington paid tribute to her generosity and her work, which he called "a business we should all be proud of."

At the next NNBL convention, held in Philadelphia a few weeks later, Washington invited Walker to serve as principal speaker. As she walked regally to the podium, he said, "I now take pleasure in introducing to the convention one of the most progressive and successful businesswomen of our race—Madam C. J. Walker."

When Walker concluded her speech, Washington thanked her for "all she has done for our race." Then he added a note Walker must have relished. "You talk about what the men are doing in a business way," he said. "Why, if we don't watch out, the women will excel us!"

That was exactly what Madam Walker intended to do. ✿

2

A HARDWORKING
CHILDHOOD

MADAM C. J. WALKER was born Sarah Breedlove on a Delta, Louisiana, cotton plantation on December 23, 1867. She was the first member of her family to be born free. Perhaps her parents, former slaves Owen and Minerva Breedlove, hoped that her Christmas-season birth was a message of good fortune, a sign that her life would be better than theirs. Optimism, however, could not have come easily to the Breedloves.

The 1867 cotton crop, attacked by bollworms just before harvest time, had been a disaster. When Christmas arrived, the Breedloves had no money to buy presents for Sarah's brother and sister, Alex and Louvenia. Sarah was the family's special and only gift.

Owen and Minerva Breedlove, who were probably born during the 1830s, worked as field hands on Robert W. Burney's Madison Parish (county) cotton plantation. Crops, especially cotton, flourished in the dark, rich soil deposited by the Mississippi River; by 1861, when the Civil War began, Madison Parish had become one of the South's most prosperous farming areas. Because raising and harvesting cotton

Walker was born Sarah Breedlove in this one-room cabin in Delta, Louisiana, in 1867. She was the first member of her family to start life as a free American citizen.

required many hands, local planters had acquired slaves in great numbers; blacks in the parish outnumbered whites by almost 10 to 1.

Burney's thousand-acre plantation, one of many that lined this stretch of the Mississippi, included a sprawling manor house nestled among giant oaks and fragrant magnolias. Known as Grand View, the estate offered a sweeping panorama of the bustling city of Vicksburg, across the river in Mississippi.

Steamboats from New Orleans, Memphis, St. Louis, and Louisville plied Vicksburg's harbor, delivering passengers and merchandise on the city's teeming docks and picking up cotton for cloth factories in New England and Europe. Adding to Vicksburg's clatter were the clanking, puffing trains that carried passengers and products east and the ferry boats, their steam whistles hooting, that shuttled goods and people between Vicksburg and Delta.

Vicksburg's location made it a strategic prize during the Civil War. In 1862, Union general Ulysses S. Grant laid siege to the city, hoping to cut communication and supply routes between the Confederacy's eastern and western regions. Grant anchored his gunboats just off Grand View, and used the plantation itself as a battle-staging area.

In an attempt to divert the Mississippi from Vicksburg's strategic bluffs, Union engineers even began to dig a canal through Grand View. The canal project failed, but after almost a year of Union bombardment, the entrenched Confederate forces yielded Vicksburg on July 4, 1863, marking one of the greatest Union victories of the war.

Less than two years later, on April 9, 1865, the South surrendered. The war was over. Like much of the South, Delta lay in ruins, its homes, crops, and livestock destroyed by Union soldiers. Although some newly freed slaves left the plantations, Owen and Minerva Breedlove stayed because they had no other way to support themselves.

Plantation owners, who controlled local govern-
ments and state legislatures, often prevented former
slaves from buying farmland. After the crop failure of
1867, the federal government ordered black farmers
to accept any work they were offered or face arrest for
vagrancy. To protect themselves, the Breedloves
continued to work for the family that had once
owned them, receiving acreage, seed, and tools in
return for a share of the crops they raised.

The sharecropping system almost always worked
out to the tenants' great disadvantage. Tenants were
forced to buy their supplies from the landlord and to
process their crops with the landlord's equipment, all
at prices he established. At the end of each season of
backbreaking labor, "croppers" usually owed their
employers more than they had earned. For most, the
system amounted to a second bondage.

Unable to afford even one day without working,
Minerva Breedlove chopped cotton right up to the
day of Sarah's birth. She bore her third child in the
drafty, one-room cabin she shared with her family.
Although the fireplace at one end provided heat and
light, the cabin's roof leaked, and wind whistled
through the wooden shutters on its glassless windows.
The Breedloves wanted their children to have more
than this. They craved education for their offspring
because literacy was a symbol of freedom; themselves
illiterate, they dreamed of sending Sarah and her
siblings to school.

Educating them, however, proved a daunting
challenge. Schools for former slaves and their families
were scarce, and even these encountered fierce opposition from racists. Refusing to accept blacks' legal
right to education, the Ku Klux Klan, the Knights of
the White Camellia, the White Brotherhood, and
other southern white-supremist groups often burned
down black schoolhouses and harassed and even
murdered their teachers and pupils.

Another barrier to education for black plantation

*Like the child pictured here,
Walker went to work in the
cotton fields at an early age.
Sharecroppers' daughters enjoyed
little free time: Along with their
mothers, they cooked in the
morning, planted and harvested
all day, tended the family
livestock in the evening, and on
Saturday, washed mountains of
laundry for white customers.*

families was time. Children worked alongside their parents in the cotton fields, leaving only the short periods before planting and after harvesting for school. Sarah probably started working in the fields, carrying water for the older laborers, when she was about five years old. She soon graduated to planting, dropping seeds in the long furrows made by the men and women who pushed the plows.

Every morning, Sarah, Louvenia, and their mother got up at sunrise to cook a breakfast of corn bread, molasses, and fried salt pork. At the same time, they started that night's dinner, preparing the vegetables that would simmer all day in an iron pot. Watching her mother and older sister carefully, Sarah learned quickly. In the evenings, she dug potatoes from the garden, swept the yard, and fed the chickens—whose eggs the family sold for extra pennies.

Saturdays were for laundry, washed in large wooden tubs on the riverbank. From dawn until dark, Sarah, Louvenia, and Minerva Breedlove used wooden sticks and washboards to beat the soil out of their own clothes and those of the white customers who paid them about one dollar per week.

In its own way, laundering was as hard as picking cotton. The huge linen sheets and tablecloths of the Breedloves' customers were heavy and difficult to handle, especially after being soaked in boiling water and strong lye soap. Still, Sarah would recall later, she loved to listen to her mother and the other women sing while they washed; their harmony and rhythm seemed to make some of the job's drudgery evaporate.

Sarah probably heard the older women talk about slavery and their dreams of a better life. Sometimes, when the women's voices blended with the steamboat whistles from the river, Sarah would imagine herself traveling. But most of the time, she and the others simply worked hard.

The combination of endless labor, poor diet, and almost nonexistent medical care left most of the sharecroppers with little resistance to illness. Malaria and yellow fever stalked the hot, humid communities on the Mississippi's banks, regularly taking their toll of women, men, and children. In 1874, when Sarah was seven years old, a particularly severe outbreak of yellow fever claimed many lives in Delta; two of those fatally stricken were Owen and Minerva Breedlove.

Sarah missed her parents terribly, but in the general suffering of the community, her sorrows were overlooked. No one seemed to have time to worry about one lonesome, frightened little girl. The Breedlove children tried to work the land they lived on, but without their parents, they found it impossible. Finally, Sarah's brother, Alex, decided to move to Vicksburg and look for work.

Alone on the farm, Sarah and Louvenia found life harder than ever. Sarah longed to go to school, but she and her sister spent almost all their waking moments at their washtubs, trying to make enough money to stay alive. Only at the end of her long working day did Sarah have even a few moments to call her own; whenever she could, she spent this precious time sitting on the riverbank near the cabin, inhaling the sweet smells of sassafras and flowering plum trees.

On these evenings, she looked across the water at Vicksburg, watching the copper sunlight dance on the windows of the city's elegant homes and long warehouses. She loved to meet the ferry and gaze at the women travelers in their beautiful hats and expensive clothes, so different from her own patched and faded dress.

In 1878, yellow fever struck again. Between July and November, more than 3,000 people around Vicksburg died in the region's worst epidemic yet. To make matters worse, the cotton crop failed that year.

With no work and no money, thousands of blacks, including the Breedlove girls, lost their homes.

They had no choice but to move across the river, where Louvenia hoped she could find work as a washerwoman or servant. Many other Louisiana blacks made the same decision, streaming into Vicksburg in a steady tide. At about this time, the black population—poor, out of work, and in constant dread of the Ku Klux Klan and other racist bands—began to look with interest at a movement known as Afro-American nationalism, or separatism.

Some separatists believed that America's blacks should form all-black colonies outside the United States, particularly in Africa. Others urged their followers to set up new black communities in the

An 1870s photograph shows Vicksburg, Mississippi, which became home for the 11-year-old Walker and her older sister, Louvenia, in 1878. Orphaned and friendless, the two girls made a meager living by washing clothes for wealthy whites.

American West, which promised economic opportunity to people of all races.

Soon after Sarah and Louvenia arrived in Vicksburg, they heard people talking about Dr. Collins, a traveling preacher. Visiting towns along the Mississippi, Collins assured blacks that a ship would soon come to carry them to Africa and deliver them from their "second bondage" of poverty and fear. Collins's talk of deliverance made many people think about the Bible's Moses, who led his people out of bondage and into the Promised Land.

As news of Collins's plan spread, more and more blacks gathered in the towns along the river. But no ship arrived. Stranded, the would-be emigrants further congested the area's already crowded communi-

Benjamin ("Pap") Singleton and his colleague S. A. McClure (right) prepare to board a frontier-bound riverboat in 1879. Singleton, who flooded the South with handbills (opposite page) urging blacks to move to "Sunny Kansas," led hundreds of Exodusters (black settlers) west in the late 1870s.

ties. By early 1879, however, another separatist leader appeared, this one offering a more accessible dream.

Describing Kansas as a land of cheap farmland and freedom from white oppression, black Tennessean Benjamin "Pap" Singleton urged other blacks to join him in a great exodus to the West. Hundreds did, boarding steamboats bound for St. Louis, where they took trains to the frontier. Known as Exodusters, these settlers were to establish several all-black western towns, including Bookertee, Nicodemus, and North Fork Colored.

Standing alone on a Vicksburg dock one day in 1879, 11-year-old Sarah waved as the last boat steamed upriver. She wished she were aboard, sailing away to a new life instead of sharing a drafty shack with her sister and new brother-in-law, Willie Powell, a man she would recall as cruel and contemptuous.

Three years later, Sarah escaped from the domineering Powell. At 14, "to get a home of my own," as she later put it, she married Moses McWilliams, a Vicksburg laborer. She decided his name had a good ring to it: Perhaps, like his biblical namesake, Moses would be a conductor to greener pastures. But jobs were still scarce in the Vicksburg of the 1880s. McWilliams took work where he found it, probably hauling crops to market, repairing streets and railroads, and picking cotton during the harvest season. Sarah continued to work as a washerwoman, as she had since she was a little girl in Delta.

On June 6, 1885, when she was 17, Sarah gave birth to a daughter; she and her husband named their little girl Lelia. Now Sarah was busier than ever, but she was content. If she worked hard enough, she thought, she could someday make Lelia's life easier than her own. Soon after Lelia's second birthday, however, Moses McWilliams was killed in an accident.

At 20, Sarah was suddenly a widow and a single mother. She had no intention of rejoining her sister and brother-in-law, but how could she manage on her own? Discussing her problem with neighbors, Sarah learned that there were jobs for laundresses in St. Louis, where wages were higher than those in Vicksburg. Several acquaintances told Sarah that they had relatives in St. Louis who took in boarders.

All her life, Sarah Breedlove McWilliams had listened to train whistles echoing through the night. With hungry eyes, she had watched steamboats disappear around the river bend to new and exciting places. It was time, she decided, to move on. With a baby on her hip and a boat ticket in her hand, she boarded a northbound riverboat. No matter what the future brought, she told herself, it had to be better than the past. **⟨⟩**

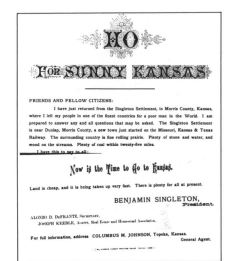

3

"I GOT MYSELF A START BY GIVING MYSELF A START"

S ARAH McWILLIAMS WATCHED her daughter skip off to school and smiled. Giving Lelia what she lacked herself—an education—made all her sacrifices seem worthwhile.

When the little girl disappeared from view, McWilliams walked through her St. Louis rooming-house hallway to the backyard. There, clustered around the rickety porch, stood her wooden washtubs. Years later, she remembered the moment: "As I bent over the washboard and looked at my arms buried in the soapsuds, I said to myself, 'What are you going to do when you grow old and your back gets stiff?' This set me to thinking, but with all my thinking, I couldn't see how I, a poor washerwoman, was going to better my condition."

McWilliams looked at the baskets heaped with dirty clothes, then sighed and wiped her hands on her long, checkered apron. She raised an arm to her forehead, wiped the sweat with her sleeve, and pushed back her calico bandanna. She knew her life was better than it had been when she left Vicksburg six years ago. Still, sometimes she could not help feeling discouraged.

When Walker arrived in St. Louis, Missouri, in 1888, she joined one of the nation's largest black communities. She also became a member of the St. Paul African Methodist Episcopal Church, a congregation whose members specialized in helping the city's poor.

When she and her daughter arrived in St. Louis in 1888, McWilliams had headed for the city's black community. She found it filled with recently arrived people, many of them widowed mothers like herself. In this Mississippi River city of almost half a million residents lived one of the country's largest black populations, some 35,000 people. Swelled by migrants from the Deep South, the black community supported 3 weekly newspapers and more than 100 businesses.

St. Louis's pace was far swifter than Vicksburg's. Hurrying along its clamorous, electric- and gas-lighted streets were white and black Missouri natives, transplanted easterners, and European immigrants. Dress styles ranged from ragged to elegant; vehicles included everything from expensive horse-drawn carriages to shabby peddlers' wagons. By the 1890s, the city would claim the nation's largest brewery, its most important drug manufacturer, and its biggest tobacco factory.

Along the St. Louis riverfront, noisy, brightly lighted saloons and cafés attracted nightly crowds of gamblers, hustlers, and prostitutes. Ragtime, the infectious, syncopated piano music that seemed to come from the heart of black St. Louis, poured from dance halls and bars. People tapped their feet to the rhythms of such popular tunes as "Ragtime Millionaire," with lyrics that captured the hopes and ironic humor of the community: "I'm afraid I may die of money disease / Don't bother a minute about what those white folks care / I'm a ragtime millionaire!"

McWilliams could not imagine herself a millionaire, but she had no trouble in finding work as a washerwoman. It was hard labor and carried no status, but it was better than working as a live-in servant, her only other option. Washing clothes at home meant she could keep an eye on Lelia.

Taking pride in her work, McWilliams carefully scrubbed out spots, added just the right amount of

A laundress scrubs clothes in her backyard tubs. Although Walker continued to hope for a bright future, she sometimes gave in to despair: "I couldn't see," she said, "how I, a poor washerwoman, was going to better my condition."

starch, thoroughly cleaned the rust from her irons, and painstakingly pressed the delicate lace and ruffles of her customers' clothes. When she delivered her laundry, she walked with dignity, a basket of neatly folded clothes balanced atop her head.

McWilliams's delivery route often led her across the Eads Bridge, which spanned the Mississippi River and led to East St. Louis, Illinois. As she walked, she later remembered, she often marveled at the skill of the engineers who had built this great brick-and-steel structure. There must be a way, she had thought, to build a bridge to prosperity for herself and Lelia. In her prayers, she asked God to show her the way.

McWilliams believed God would help her; she also knew she would have to help herself. Working long hours over her steaming tubs, scrimping on necessities, doing without luxuries, she managed to put aside a little money each week. By the time Lelia graduated from high school, her proud mother was able to send her to Knoxville College, a small black institution in Knoxville, Tennessee.

At about this time, McWilliams married again. Little is known of her second husband, John Davis; McWilliams rarely spoke of him except to remark that he was a heavy drinker. She apparently divorced him before her daughter went away to college.

Soon after her move to St. Louis, McWilliams had joined the St. Paul African Methodist Episcopal Church. Established in 1840, St. Paul was the first St. Louis church planned, built, and financed by blacks. Defying the pre–Civil War laws that forbade blacks to learn to read and write, St. Paul sponsored a secret school for its members, and it had long extended its aid to newcomers to the city, helping them find houses and jobs, and supplying them with clothing and other necessities.

The women of the church had proved both friendly and generous to McWilliams. Deeply grateful, she vowed to help others in turn, although she had little money to contribute. After she settled into city life, she joined the Mite Missionary Society, the St. Paul organization that assisted needy members of the community.

Years later, a newspaper article described McWilliams's first activity for the society: "She read in the [St. Louis] *Post-Dispatch* . . . of an aged colored man with a blind sister and an invalid wife depending on him for support. Without acquaintance of any kind with the family, she went among friends

The Eads Bridge forms a backdrop for St. Louis's bustling riverfront in the 1890s. The sight was a familiar one to Walker, who often crossed the bridge with a load of laundry on her head.

in the behalf of the distressed people, succeeding in collecting $3.60 which she gave to them. . . . She felt it was her duty to do even more [so] she arranged for a pound party through which means groceries in abundance were given, also a purse of $7.50."

Among the missionary society's members were a number of prominent, well-educated black women. Through them, McWilliams encountered a new world, peopled with prosperous, cultured blacks. She was dazzled by their stylish dress and formal manners and awed by their ability to organize themselves and become community leaders.

McWilliams was even more impressed by the black leaders who came to St. Louis for the 1904 World's Fair. Mingling with dazzled fairgoers were such luminaries as poet Paul Laurence Dunbar, scholar and political activist W. E. B. Du Bois, and newspaper publisher T. Thomas Fortune. Even the great Booker T. Washington was there, delivering two speeches to spellbound black audiences.

Also taking part in the festivities were 200 delegates of the National Association of Colored Women (NACW). After a meeting at St. Paul church, the NACW members proceeded to the fair, where they listened to an address by Margaret Murray Washington (the wife of Booker T.). Local newspapers ran Washington's picture and reported on her speech, marking the first time that the white St. Louis press had featured positive coverage of any black woman.

Gazing at the immaculately groomed Margaret Washington, Sarah McWilliams reflected on her own appearance. Perhaps, she thought, if she improved it, she might gain some of the self-confidence exuded by Washington and other successful black women. McWilliams always wore neat, crisply starched clothing, the better to advertise her skills as a laundress, but she was self-conscious about her hair;

When Margaret Murray Washington, wife of Booker T. Washington, addressed the St. Louis branch of the National Association of Colored Women in 1904, Walker watched in awe. Washington's calm elegance inspired the 37-year-old laundress to improve her own appearance, starting with her sparse and damaged hair.

broken and patchy, it revealed her scalp in several places.

Countless black women shared McWilliams's hair problems. Sometimes inadequate diets, stress, and poor health caused hair loss; sometimes it was the result of lotions and treatments containing harmful chemicals. Advertisements for hair improvement products—Queen Pomade, La Creole Hair Restorer, Kinkilla, and Ford's Original Ozonized Ox Marrow, for example—crowded the pages of black newspapers.

The manufacturer of Thomas's Magic Hair Grower claimed its product would "cleanse the scalp of dandruff, stop it from falling, and make it grow even on bald spots." Because many blacks looked down on hair straightening as imitative of whites, Thomas's ads stressed that its product was "NOT A STRAIGHTENER." Although they disdained copying white females, few black women wore the traditional hairstyles and elaborate ornaments of their African foremothers, and many yearned for long hair.

The "ideal" American woman of the 1890s had a full bosom, a tiny waist, and a great mass of hair, which she swept to the top of her head. Although not many women of any race could meet all these beauty standards, most tried for lengthy tresses. Women whose hair refused to grow long wore wigs and hairpieces.

Sarah McWilliams asked God to keep her hair from falling out. She also tried a number of patented hair mixtures, including the Poro Company's Wonderful Hair Grower, but with little success. The St. Louis–based Poro Company hired local women to sell its products door to door; for a few months McWilliams worked as a sales agent when she was not washing clothes. Then she got a better idea: If she could devise her own hair product, one that really worked for her, she could go into business for herself.

Sketched by artist Charles Dana Gibson, this trio represented turn-of-the-century Americans' ideal woman: wasp waisted, full bosomed, and crowned with long, upswept hair. Few women, black or white, could achieve a "Gibson girl" figure, but most either grew their hair long or wore a hairpiece.

In early 1905, McWilliams informed friends that, with divine help, she had learned how to make the mixture she wanted. God, she later told a reporter, "answered my prayer, for one night I had a dream, and in that dream a big black man appeared to me and told me what to mix up for my hair. Some of the remedy was grown in Africa, but I sent for it, mixed it, put it on my scalp, and in a few weeks my hair was coming in faster than it had ever fallen out. I tried it on my friends; it helped them. I made up my mind I would begin to sell it."

Perhaps because she knew she would be in direct competition with the Poro Company, McWilliams decided to leave St. Louis before starting her new business. She had made one especially good friend in the city: Charles Joseph Walker, a sales agent for a local black newspaper. Except for Walker, she had little reason to remain in Missouri; she had divorced John Davis, and Lelia was still at school in Tennessee.

Once again, McWilliams packed her belongings and headed for a new frontier, this one in Denver.

Countermen await customers in E. L. Scholtz's Denver pharmacy. Family records suggest that the Colorado druggist employed Walker as a cook and that he advised the future cosmetics tycoon about ingredients for her first products: Wonderful Hair Grower, Vegetable Shampoo, and Glossine.

Her brother had recently died, leaving his widow and four daughters in the Colorado city. McWilliams believed they could help each other. For the first time in her life, the 37-year-old woman would leave the Mississippi River area of her birth.

On July 21, 1905, McWilliams arrived at Denver's Union Depot with her savings: $1.50, about a week's pay for her work as a laundress. Colorado's mountains and wide blue skies astonished her, and she found Denver's crisp, dry air a welcome change from the steamy heat of St. Louis. Along the city's wide boulevards, cattlemen, silver miners, land speculators, and frontiersmen jockeyed for their share of the riches and adventure promised by the West.

Colorado's entire population was only slightly larger than that of St. Louis alone. When McWilliams arrived, fewer than 10,000 blacks lived in the state. Even here, where slavery had never taken root, they faced discrimination, but Colorado nevertheless offered blacks the chance to work in state and local government; many had started their own businesses.

Settling into the Mile High City, as Denver is known, McWilliams rented an attic room, joined the Shorter Chapel African Methodist Episcopal Church, and found a job as a cook. According to family records, her employer was probably E. L. Scholtz, a Canadian-born druggist who owned the largest, best-equipped pharmacy west of Chicago. His drugstore compounded both doctors' prescriptions and home medical remedies and tonics.

McWilliams probably consulted Scholtz about ingredients for the hair preparations she was concocting. In any case, she spent her evenings working on her formulas and testing them on herself and her nieces. Finally, she came up with three products that met her requirements. She called them Wonderful Hair Grower, Glossine, and Vegetable Shampoo.

McWilliams saved her money carefully; before long, she could afford to leave her cook's job. To pay her rent, she took in laundry two days each week; the rest of the time she spent in mixing her products and selling them door to door. As a saleswoman, she usually wore a long, dark skirt and a white blouse; she carried her goods in a trim black case.

McWilliams soon proved herself a natural marketer, introducing her products with free demonstrations. After thoroughly washing a woman's hair with her Vegetable Shampoo, the saleswoman applied her Wonderful Hair Grower, a product that contained medication to combat dandruff and other conditions that sometimes caused hair loss. To complete the treatment, McWilliams applied a light oil to the customer's hair, then pressed it with a heated metal comb. This procedure softened the tight curls characterizing the hair of many people of African descent.

McWilliams had targeted her market well: Denver's black women began buying her wares with enthusiasm. At first, she used all her profits for raw materials and advertising. Her ads in the *Colorado Statesman*, a black newspaper published in Denver, generated mail orders, and her personal sales trips produced heartening results.

But McWilliams's best advertisement was herself. A customer who looked at a "before" picture, and then at the saleswoman herself, could hardly fail to be impressed. When McWilliams announced that her long, well-groomed hair was the product of her treatments, the customer was almost sure to place an order.

McWilliams, who had stayed in touch with her St. Louis friend, Charles Joseph Walker, wrote to him about her growing business. After providing a steady stream of advice by mail, Walker, known to all as C.J., showed up in Denver in person. Already fond of each other, the two soon decided to marry; their wedding ceremony took place on January 4, 1906.

Familiar with newspaper promotion campaigns, Walker helped his wife expand her mail-order business. Together, they manufactured and sold such products as C. J. Walker's Blood and Rheumatic Remedy and the newly named Madam C. J. Walker's Wonderful Hair Grower.

Sarah Walker began calling herself Madam not only to identify her marital status but to give her products more appeal. The title also evoked thoughts of the world's fashion and beauty capital, France, where married women were called Madame. In the United States of the 1890s, women had few guaranteed legal rights; they could not vote, and in most states, could not even own property. Worse off, of course, were black women, who were frequently stereotyped as childlike and ignorant. Thus, many black women in the public eye, such as opera singer Madame Lillian Evanti, adopted the title to convey an image of worth and dignity.

By the time the Walkers' business was bringing in $10 per week, C. J. Walker decided it had reached its full potential. Not so his wife: Sarah Walker believed that if they only knew about it, women all over the country would buy her Wonderful Hair Grower. Accordingly, she made plans for an extended sales trip.

Her husband and other advisers predicted she would not even earn enough to pay her expenses. She left anyway, setting out in September 1906 for what would become a year and a half of traveling to nine states, including Oklahoma, Louisiana, Mississippi, and New York. Within a few months, she was making weekly sales of $35, more than twice the salary of the average white American male worker, and 20 times that of the average black woman worker.

By this time, Lelia, now 21 years old, had graduated from college. She moved to Denver to help run the mail-order business while her mother traveled. Elegantly dressed, nearly six feet tall, and regal of bearing, Lelia gave the company added distinction. She also demonstrated a flair for business, but even with the help of her four cousins, Anjetta, Thirsapen, Mattie, and Gladis, she could barely keep up with the orders her mother kept pouring in.

On the road, Sarah Walker was doing more than selling; she was training agents who could demonstrate and take orders for Walker products in return for a share of the profits. By the spring of 1908, she had signed on dozens of representatives and brought her company's monthly income to a breathtaking $400. Running a now vast mail-order operation, she decided to move her company closer to the nation's population centers.

After a visit to Pittsburgh, Walker selected the Pennsylvania city as her new base of operations. A thriving industrial and banking center, Pittsburgh boasted a sophisticated transportation system, a convenient source of steel for Walker's pressing combs, and a rapidly increasing black population.

In Pittsburgh, Walker rented an office on Wylie Avenue, the main street of the city's black community. She shared the bustling neighborhood with 45 churches, 5 lawyers, 22 doctors, and dozens of businesses, including tailor shops, restaurants, funeral

Vegetable Shampoo, one of the Walker company's most popular offerings, promised to ease dandruff and other scalp problems. Most manufacturers of black hair-care products promoted their wares with light-skinned models, but Walker—correctly assuming that customers would respond to a woman who looked more like them—used her own likeness on packages and ads.

parlors, and pharmacies. The area was home to a number of prosperous black families, but most of the city's blacks worked in service jobs or as laborers.

Although the bulk of Pittsburgh's mining and manufacturing jobs went to newly arrived European immigrants, waves of black southerners poured steadily into the city, eager to take whatever work they could find. Businesswoman Walker saw the influx of blacks as a source of new agents and customers.

In the summer of 1908, Sarah Walker's daughter joined her in Pittsburgh. Together, the women opened a beauty parlor and a training school for Walker agents, which they called Lelia College. A graduate from the school would be known, they decided, as a hair culturist.

Word of the new college spread quickly. Applying for entrance were housekeepers, office cleaners, laundresses, and even schoolteachers, women whose needs and dreams Walker understood well. Over the next two years, Lelia College turned out scores of hair culturists, most of whom were delighted with their new careers.

In a letter to Walker, one graduate said, "You have opened up a trade for hundreds of colored women to make an honest and profitable living where they make as much in one week as a month's salary would bring from any other position that a colored woman can secure."

In 1910, the *Pennsylvania Negro Business Directory* ran a feature story about Walker, whom it called "one of the most successful businesswomen of the race in this community." Accompanying the article was a photograph of Walker, showing a woman dramatically changed in the course of only a few years. Posed with her hands clasped behind her back and her long hair pinned atop her head, Walker looked confident and dignified. Her high-necked,

A 1910 photograph of the 43-year-old Walker shows a serene, fashionably attired woman, strikingly different in appearance from the neat but shabbily dressed laundress of earlier days.

lace-bodiced gown more closely resembled her former customers' clothing than the threadbare gingham dresses she had worn during her days as a laundress.

As she rose in her career, Walker found herself sought out by the city's most prominent black citizens, including clergymen and the women who headed community and church organizations. The kind of people she had once admired from afar were now admiring her.

4

GEARING UP

❧

Pittsburgh provided fertile ground for the early growth of Madam C. J. Walker's business. During the two years she spent in the booming Pennsylvania city, Walker trained scores of hair culturists at Lelia College and turned her mail-order and door-to-door operations into a profitable business. Still, she felt restless.

Despite Pittsburgh's commercial potential, Walker yearned for broader horizons; by 1910, she was scouting for a new city in which to establish a permanent national headquarters. When she visited Indianapolis, Indiana, in February, she decided she had found the spot. Sometimes called the Crossroads of America, the midwestern city was situated at the heart of the nation's transportation network, a major asset for a mail-order operation. Also attractive to Walker was Indianapolis's thriving black business community.

Although Indianapolis lacked a major waterway, it had become the country's largest inland manufacturing center because of its access to eight major railway systems. More than 1 million freight cars passed through the city's rail yards annually, and nearly 200 passenger trains arrived and departed daily.

In the first two decades of the 20th century, Indianapolis was the center of America's automobile

Moving from Pittsburgh to Indianapolis in 1910, Walker swung into high gear: She legally incorporated her business, opened a factory, and started assembling the dedicated and talented staff that would help turn her company into one of the nation's top black-owned enterprises.

43

industry; in 1909, the city built the Indianapolis Speedway. (Originally designed to test-drive cars, the Speedway became a racecourse after the first Indy 500 race in 1911.) The city was also home to scores of large manufacturing and industrial companies.

When he met Walker on her first visit to his city, Indianapolis newspaper executive George L. Knox strongly advised her to settle there. Knox, who published *The Freeman*, one of the nation's most widely read black newspapers, backed his argument for Indianapolis by telling Walker his own story.

Born a slave in 1841, he had arrived in Indianapolis in 1864. After spending some years apprenticed to a black barber, he opened his own 10-chair barbershop in one of the city's large hotels. Knox used his access to his wealthy white customers to advance himself economically and politically; by the late 1890s, he had become the city's leading black businessman and the state's most powerful black Republican.

His own success, Knox assured Walker, was by no means unique in Indianapolis. The black community's main thoroughfares, Indiana Avenue and North West Street, were lined with thriving businesses: cafés, offices, and such assorted enterprises as Belle Davis's catering firm, Oliver Martin's coal company, and Archie Greathouse's saloon and restaurant.

Knox probably also mentioned H. L. Sanders, a former hotel waiter who had become America's most prosperous black uniform manufacturer. At the time of Walker's visit, Sanders, his wife, and their 25 employees were producing uniforms and work clothes for hospital aides, hotel workers, janitors, and domestic employees across the nation.

After noting the natural assets of Indianapolis and observing the civic pride of Knox and other Indianapolis boosters, Walker made up her mind. "I was so impressed with [Indianapolis] and the cordial welcome extended," she said later, "that I decided to make this city my home."

Leaving her 24-year-old daughter—who had married John Robinson, a Pittsburgh hotel worker, in 1909—in charge of the company's Pittsburgh operations, Walker moved to Indianapolis with her husband in the spring of 1910. Shortly after she settled in, Knox introduced her to another recent arrival, a young black attorney named Robert Lee Brokenburr. Born in 1886 in Hampton (then Phoebus), Virginia, Brokenburr had attended Hampton Institute—Booker T. Washington's alma mater—and graduated from the Howard University Law School in 1909.

At Knox's recommendation, Walker hired Brokenburr as a part-time legal adviser. In September 1911, he filed articles of incorporation for the Madam C. J. Walker Manufacturing Company, a corporation that would "manufacture and sell a hairgrowing, beautifying and scalp disease–curing preparation and clean scalps with the same."

Listed as the new company's officers were Walker, her husband, and her daughter. Walker, who hoped Brokenburr would work for her full time, asked the young lawyer to serve as acting president and treasurer of the company's board of directors. More interested in law than business, he declined the offer.

During her travels, Walker had met another young attorney, Freeman Briley Ransom. Born in Grenada, Mississippi, in 1882, Ransom had studied at Columbia University Law School, moved to Indianapolis in 1911, and set up his own law office. In exchange for room and board in Walker's home, he gave her free legal advice.

As her travel schedule became heavier, Walker realized she needed someone with legal expertise to oversee her company's day-to-day operations. After much discussion, she persuaded Ransom to sign on as general manager and attorney; still maintaining his

Robert Lee Brokenburr, a graduate of Howard University, started working for Walker in 1910. Soon afterward, the 24-year-old Virginia-born attorney filed articles of incorporation for the Madam C. J. Walker Manufacturing Company, a business that would make and sell "a hairgrowing, beautifying and scalp disease–curing preparation and clean scalps with the same."

Lelia College graduate Alice Kelly was a Kentucky schoolteacher when she met Walker in 1911. Spotting the self-assured young woman as an ideal employee, Walker hired her, sent her to Indianapolis, and soon named her forewoman of the Walker company's bustling factory.

private law practice, Brokenburr agreed to become the company's assistant manager.

Brokenburr and Ransom frequently disagreed on political and philosophical issues, but they respected each other and worked well as a business team. And, like many young black professionals of the time, they shared a sense of pioneering; Walker knew she could count on them to protect her business interests while she was traveling.

With her daily operations now under firm control, she began focusing her attention on the company's future, seeking skilled people to help her expand it. Everywhere she went, she recruited new Walker agents and employees for her main office. On one southern sales trip, she met Alice Kelly, a teacher at Kentucky's Eckstein Norton Institute. Impressed with the younger woman's decisive, confident manner, Walker offered her a job.

Kelly learned quickly, and Walker soon named her forewoman of the Indianapolis factory. Walker also hired one of Kelly's former students, Violet Davis Reynolds, as her private secretary. So impressed was Walker with the tall, self-assured Kelly, in fact, that she even entrusted her with the company's secret hair-grower formula, until then known only by Walker and her daughter.

Kelly's strong-willed personality—and the fact that she knew the secret formula—created tension between her and Ransom. Aware of the conflict between her two top executives, Walker urged them to settle their differences. "They worked that out," another Walker employee recalled years later, "because they knew they'd have to get along to do what Madam wanted them to do."

The more successful Walker became, the more she wanted to improve her communications skills. Acutely aware of her own lack of formal education, she sought the cultured Kelly's advice on social etiquette, penmanship, public speaking, letter writing, and literature. Acting as both traveling companion and tutor, Kelly often accompanied her boss on sales trips.

Walker continued her lessons at home and in her Indianapolis office. Each morning, as she sat at her desk reading the newspapers, she asked secretary Reynolds or bookkeepers Lucy Flint and Marie Overstreet to look up unfamiliar words in the dictionary. Thus, as she educated herself, she educated her staff; she knew that her company's continued success depended on knowledgeable employees.

Walker's many sales trips, as well as her extensive advertising campaigns in the nation's black newspapers, brought daily product orders from all over the United States. Walker got especially good results from the advertisements she placed in George Knox's widely circulated paper, *The Freeman.*

C. J. Walker, an experienced newspaper sales agent, probably designed his wife's most effective ad, one that described Walker's business success and included testimonials from satisfied customers and company agents. The Walker advertisements stood out from those of other hair-care companies because they included dramatic photographs showing Walker before and after using her most popular product, Wonderful Hair Grower.

Within a year of her arrival in Indianapolis, Walker announced a set of impressive statistics: Her company now had 950 agents nationwide and a monthly income of $1,000. She put her profits back into the business, expanding her factory and hiring new employees. Situated in the heart of the city's black community, the Walker company employed neighborhood women almost exclusively. After an intensive training program in hair and beauty culture, the graduates served a stream of eager customers, giving them scalp treatments, restyling their hair,

As Walker's private secretary, Violet Davis Reynolds did more than type, file, and take dictation; her responsibilities also included helping her boss acquire the education she had missed. Whenever Walker came across an unfamiliar word, she asked Reynolds and other office workers to look it up, thus broadening the knowledge of all concerned.

F. B. Ransom, Walker's general manager, checks out an order in his Indianapolis office. Starting his association with Walker as a part-time lawyer, Ransom would eventually become her second-in-command and most trusted adviser.

and administering manicures and massages.

Always serious about her work, Walker also found time for culture and amusement. She became a patron of the arts, often hosting concerts and poetry readings, and she gradually filled her home with art objects. On her walls hung oil paintings she had commissioned from black artists; in her parlor stood a mahogany baby grand piano, along with a custom-made phonograph and a harp, both covered with gold leaf. Walker often spent her evenings listening to recorded music, reading in her library, or playing Flinch, a popular card game of the day, with friends.

Fascinated by the era's grand theaters and thrilling silent films, Walker had also become an enthusiastic moviegoer; among her favorites were Charlie Chaplin's comedies and the elaborate epics of director Cecil B. De Mille. One afternoon, however, Walker's expectation of a pleasant hour at the cinema turned to disappointment and anger.

Arriving at Indianapolis's Isis Theatre, she gave the ticket seller a dime, standard admission price at the time. The agent pushed the coin back across the counter. The price, she said, was now 25 cents. Responding to Walker's quizzical look, the seller explained that the admission price had gone up—but only for "colored persons."

Furious, Walker went home and instructed attorney Ransom to sue the theater. He duly filed a complaint, accusing the Isis and its agents of practicing "unwarranted discrimination because of the color of this plaintiff" and asking for the imposition of a $100 fine. (No further records of the suit exist; the theater probably settled the complaint out of court.)

Walker, who rarely took half measures, next sent for an architect. For some time, she had been thinking about building a larger factory and office building. Now she decided to begin work at once. Completed some years later, the Walker Building would cover an entire block in downtown Indianapolis—and would include an elegant movie theater specifically operated for the city's black residents.

Few members of Indianapolis's black population—about 10 percent of the city's 233,650 people in 1919—escaped encounters with discrimination. Obviously, Walker was no exception, but her wealth and prominence gave her entrée into some areas closed to most blacks. The city's bankers, for example, treated her cordially—as they would treat any customer who deposited thousands of dollars each year. Recognizing her efficiently run company as a solid investment, Indianapolis banks willingly lent her money for expansion.

Walker also received a warm welcome in the city's department stores and automobile showrooms. One white jeweler, apparently color-blinded by Walker's purchases of silverware and diamonds, made it a point to rush out of his shop and greet her whenever he saw her car arrive.

Although she enjoyed driving herself, Walker employed a chauffeur to take her on pleasure trips.

On summer evenings, she sat in the backseat of her luxurious automobile with Alice Kelly or her nieces, Anjetta and Thirsapen Breedlove, as her driver piloted the car around Indianapolis. Gliding past the expensive homes on the city's north side, then through the industrial districts, the chauffeur maneuvered the vehicle through streets crowded with horses and wagons, automobiles, bicycles, streetcars, and the electric trains known as interurbans.

Once To Every Woman

The Isis Theatre, a popular Indianapolis movie palace, established a new admissions policy in 1912: White patrons would continue to pay a dime, but the price for "colored persons" went up to a quarter. Outraged, movie-lover Walker immediately sued the Isis for "unwarranted discrimination."

In the midst of her success, Walker began to have serious disagreements with her husband about control of the company and plans for its expansion. Business differences spilled over into the couple's personal life, finally resulting in an agreement to end the marriage. Sarah Walker filed for divorce in late 1912, but she would retain her husband's name for the rest of her life. Ironically, C. J. Walker remained a Walker agent for the rest of his life.

5

LADY BOUNTIFUL

❧

AFTER HER DIVORCE, Walker became even
more involved in her company, which, by the end of
1912, employed some 1,600 agents and produced
weekly—instead of monthly—revenues of nearly
$1,000. Meanwhile, Walker's daughter—recently di-
vorced but now known as A'Lelia Walker
Robinson—was beginning to extend the company's
East Coast operation into New York City.

On one of her frequent visits to Indianapolis,
A'Lelia Robinson noticed 13-year-old Mae Bryant, a
neighborhood girl who sometimes ran errands for the
Walker enterprises. Because Mae had long, thick
hair, Robinson thought she would make an excellent
model for Walker products.

Etta Bryant, a poor widow who had recently
moved to Indianapolis with her children, agreed to
let her daughter model. As the Walker women came
to know Mae better, they realized she was not only a
good-natured but an unusually bright child, one who
might benefit from the advantages their wealth could
provide.

Mae spent more and more time with the Walkers.
Eventually, the childless Robinson asked Etta Bryant
to let her adopt Mae. She would, she assured Bryant,

*Seated in the back of their elegant touring car, Walker (right) and
her daughter, A'Lelia, prepare to take a spin around town.
Although she was an excellent driver, Walker usually rode behind
her chauffeur, Otho Patton.*

Long-haired Mae Bryant was 13 years old when A'Lelia Walker Robinson hired her as a model for Walker products. Charmed by the bright, attractive young woman, Robinson eventually adopted her, providing Walker with her only grandchild.

give the girl a good education and be sure she kept in constant touch with her family in Indianapolis. Aware that Robinson could give Mae much more than she herself could, Bryant consented to the adoption.

When Robinson returned to Pittsburgh, Mae went with her. And when Walker came through on her sales trips, she often picked Mae up, taking her along to learn the business. With her new granddaughter, Walker spent much of the summer of 1912 along the East Coast and in the upper southern states, giving lectures and promoting business at conventions held by black religious, fraternal, and civic organizations.

After each lecture, Walker asked her audience to endorse her as the "foremost colored businesswoman in America," a title she hoped would give her an edge over her competitors. Most of the groups obliged willingly.

In July 1912, Walker attended the annual conference of the National Association of Colored Women, held in Hampton, Virginia. There she met Mary McLeod Bethune, the 37-year-old founder of the Daytona Normal and Industrial Institute for Negro Girls. Determined to bring schooling to a Florida area that offered blacks no education at all, Bethune had struggled to open her tiny institute in 1904. By 1912, the school, at that point accepting boys as well as girls and known as the Daytona Educational Industrial Training School, had expanded vastly.

Impressed by Bethune and her work with black youngsters, Walker volunteered to lead a fund-raising effort for the school's benefit. The two women's mutual respect led to a lifelong friendship.

From Virginia, Walker continued her tireless pilgrimage, speaking and demonstrating her products at black churches, Masonic lodges, and public halls. By train and by car, she visited hundreds of communities, sometimes traveling with her nieces, sometimes with her granddaughter. The young women helped with the demonstrations and other chores, peppering each town with Walker leaflets and booklets, then signing up new Walker agents. When a community was too small for a scheduled train stop, Walker and her aides tossed company literature to the crowds waiting along the tracks.

Because telephone service at the time was limited and sometimes unreliable, Walker depended on the mail to communicate with her staff. From the road, she wrote almost daily letters to her daughter and to Ransom, instructing them on company operations, describing her sales efforts, and relating personal tidbits and details. Back in Indianapolis, each day's mail delivery brought hundreds of dollars worth of orders from Walker and her agents. In a May 1913 letter to Walker, Ransom said, "Your business is increasing here every day. I think you are the money making wonder of the age."

Ransom, who looked on himself as Walker's financial watchdog, sometimes gently scolded her for what he regarded as extravagance. In one letter to him, Walker said, "Am writing to let you know I have given a check for $1,381.50 to the Cadillac Motor Co. Won't you see to it that the check is cashed? . . . I guess you think I am crazy, but I had a chance to get just what Lelia wanted in a car. . . ." Ransom's response: "No, I don't think you crazy, but think you very hard on your bank account. I take pleasure in the fact that there can hardly be anything else for you to buy, ha, ha!!"

Convinced that the company needed a base in New York City, A'Lelia Robinson persuaded her mother to buy a house there. For its location, Robinson selected Harlem, the uptown Manhattan area then just starting to attract black residents. By the late spring of 1913, Robinson had acquired a town house on 136th Street, near Lenox Avenue,

A'Lelia Walker Robinson, who posed for this portrait around 1907, moved to New York City in 1913. Intrigued with Harlem, the city's burgeoning black community, she talked her mother into buying a house there and then turned it into a stylish residence and beauty salon. The place delighted Walker. "There is nothing to equal it," she said, "not even on Fifth Avenue."

which she turned into living quarters and a beauty salon.

Arriving in New York with Alice Kelly in the midst of the renovation, Walker was delighted with what she saw. "In regards to this house," she wrote Ransom, "you will agree with Lelia when she said that it would be [a] monument for us both. . . . The Hair Parlor beats anything I have seen anywhere, even in the best Hair Parlors of the whites. There is nothing to equal it, not even on Fifth Avenue." Walker was not alone in her admiration for her daughter's handiwork. The *Defender* called the new establishment "the most completely equipped and beautiful hair parlor that members of our Race ever had access to."

Delighted with the project or not, Walker could not stay in one place for long. She spent the rest of that summer and early fall traveling with her chauffeur, Otho Patton, in her new seven-passenger Cole touring car. This time, the Walker women hit a score of East Coast cities, including Philadelphia, Atlantic City, Baltimore, and Washington, D.C.

In the nation's capital, Walker gave speeches in 10 churches, among them the First Baptist Church in Georgetown and the downtown Metropolitan AME Church. Lecturing on "The Negro Woman in Business," she told audiences how she had achieved success through hard work and careful planning, then urged other women to follow her example and establish their own businesses.

"Now I realize that in the so-called higher walks of life, many were prone to look down upon 'hair dressers,' as they called us," she told her listeners. "They didn't have a very high opinion of our calling, so I had to go down and dignify this work, so much so that many of the best women of our race are now engaged in this line of business," she added proudly.

Walker's host in Washington was R. W. Thompson, national correspondent for *The Freeman*. "Mme

This photograph, one of a series that illustrated Walker's Text Book of Beauty Culture, *shows Alice Kelly receiving a hot-comb treatment. The hands belong to Walker herself.*

Walker," he later wrote, "is essentially a businesswoman, and no matter where she goes or on whatever errand, she talks business. She . . . never loses the opportunity to emphasize to her sisters the importance of their getting into the world of business, of acquiring a footing in the soil, making themselves financially independent and setting an example for all people of thrift, industry and the practical application of their mental training."

The more Walker traveled and the more new ideas and new people she encountered, the more possibilities she saw. On her way home from Washington, she began thinking about expanding her business overseas. People of African descent—potential customers—lived all over the world, she reasoned. Central America, the Caribbean, and South America had heavily concentrated black populations. Why not develop an international market?

After some quick research on the area, Walker sailed for the West Indies in November 1913. Five days later, she arrived in Kingston, Jamaica, with her touring car and enough products and clothes to last three months. With Jamaica as her base, she visited Cuba, Haiti, Costa Rica, and the Panama Canal Zone, demonstrating her Walker Hair Care Method just as she had done throughout the United States. And just as they had done in the United States, women flocked to see her, to buy her goods, and to sign on as her agents.

When she returned to Indianapolis in January, Walker found her office and factory employees working furiously to fill the ever-mounting product orders. To celebrate her success, she engaged entertainer Noble Sissle and invited a throng of relatives and friends to a spring dance. At Walker's home, guests admired her fine Oriental rugs and antique furniture, nibbled delicate hors d'oeuvres, and sipped punch served from a huge silver bowl. Sarah Breedlove Walker had come a long way from a sharecroppers' cabin in Louisiana.

The following summer, Walker made a whirlwind tour of the Northeast, tirelessly promoting her products and giving dozens of speeches. As usual, audiences received her with enthusiasm. "My lecture Monday night was a grand success," she wrote business manager Ransom from one New England town. "The house was packed. The people applauded so I hardly had time to talk. . . . I have been entertained two and three times a day ever since I've been here. Haven't had a day or evening to myself."

Walker, who made increasingly frequent trips to New York, liked the city better with each visit. Harlem, buzzing with politics, business, music, and theater, gave her renewed energy. She found herself sought out by the black community's most prominent residents: composer and conductor James Reese Europe, who had performed at Carnegie Hall in 1912; Fred Moore, publisher of *New York Age*; Shakespearean actor Richard B. Harrison, who had toured with

Walker's friend William Monroe Trotter (1872–1934) edited a crusading Boston newspaper, the Guardian, and founded the National Equal Rights League. Considered radical at the time, Trotter's demands for racial integration and social justice foreshadowed the national civil rights movement of the 1960s.

poet Paul Laurence Dunbar; and Philip A. Peyton, a real estate speculator whose Afro-American Realty Company had helped open Harlem to black tenants and homeowners. By 1915, Walker was spending almost as much time in New York as in Indianapolis. She began to think about moving east.

Life in the Midwest, however, continued to provide challenge and excitement. Walker's home attracted people of all political persuasions; she agreed with few entirely, but she relished the debates produced by deeply held, conflicting ideas. Among her guests in the spring of 1915, for example, was the conservative Robert Russa Moton, an associate of Booker T. Washington and president of the National Negro Business League. To ensure an evening of spirited dialogue, Walker also invited a group representing widely divergent political opinions: journalist George Knox, Indianapolis YMCA secretary Thomas Taylor, and attorneys Robert Brokenburr and F. B. Ransom.

On another spring evening, Walker received a visit from journalist and activist William Monroe Trotter. The first black member of Phi Beta Kappa, the national scholarship fraternity, Trotter had graduated from Harvard College in 1896. He became publisher and editor of the *Guardian*, a crusading Boston newspaper, and later founded the National Equal Rights League. Admired by many, Trotter had also become a center of controversy because of his opposition to Booker T. Washington's politically conservative philosophy.

Walker differed with Washington herself, particularly on the issue of women in leadership roles, but she deeply respected him as a ground-breaking educator. And although she disagreed with most of Trotter's criticisms of Washington, she admired his political activism and dedication to racial justice. No matter what their positions on the political spectrum, Walker took a broad view of all blacks who worked for what she called "the betterment of the race."

By late summer Walker was traveling again, this time to previously untapped markets in Colorado, Utah, Montana, Oregon, Washington, and California. By now, she had added an effective new dimension to her lectures: a slide show featuring illustrations of her hair-care system along with photographs of black leaders and schools and businesses founded by blacks.

Shortly after her return to headquarters, Walker made an announcement: She had decided to move to New York City. Her manufacturing operation, she said, would remain in Indianapolis under the management of Ransom, Brokenburr, and Kelly.

Walker's associates greeted her announcement with some alarm, and many tried to persuade her to reconsider. Ransom protested vigorously, insisting that the move would be too expensive, and that it would interfere with Walker's ability to run the business. But Walker had made up her mind. She wanted to live in New York, the center of progressive black thinking and activity.

The night before Walker left Indianapolis, she sat in her bedroom gazing at a faded picture of her father, thinking about how far she had come in her 48 years. As a large group of friends waited for her below, she reminisced about her arrival in Indianapolis six years earlier. Few people had heard of her then; now she was known as "the foremost businesswoman of the race."

Less than a decade earlier, Walker had been struggling to meet her own expenses. Now people called her Lady Bountiful for her contributions to orphanages, schools, and other charities. As she headed downstairs, she heard voices raised in song. The melody was "Auld Lang Syne": "Should auld acquaintance be forgot . . ." ◖◗

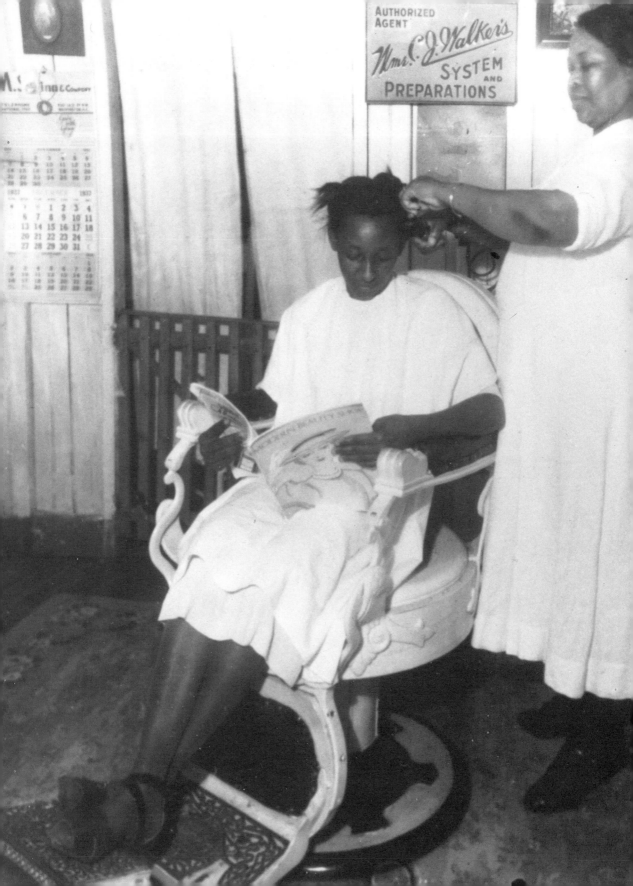

6

"DON'T SIT DOWN AND WAIT"

❧

AT THE ROOT of Madam C. J. Walker's astonishing success lay her self-confidence, boosted by her first sale and increased by those that followed. That sense of assurance, born of economic independence, impressed other women, impelling them to buy her products and to follow her example. She briskly encouraged them to do both.

Addressing the 1914 convention of the National Negro Business League, held in Muskogee, Oklahoma, Walker had said: "I am not merely satisfied in making money for myself, for I am endeavoring to provide employment for hundreds of the women of my race. I had little or no opportunity when I started out in life, having been left an orphan. . . . I had to make my own living and my own opportunity! But I made it! That is why I want to say to every Negro woman present, don't sit down and wait for the opportunities to come. . . . Get up and make them!"

Helping to make those opportunities, Walker hired black women at all levels, from factory worker to national sales agent. By 1916, she employed

Working in her home beauty salon, a Walker agent demonstrates her skills. Walker's program enabled thousands of black women to find independence and self-esteem. "I have all I can do at home," reported one agent happily, "and don't have to go out and work for white people in kitchens and factories."

20,000 agents in the United States, Central America, and the Caribbean. These women often wrote letters expressing their feelings about working for Walker: Florida agent Lizzie Bryant, for example, said, "I have all I can do at home and don't have to go out and work for white people in kitchens and factories."

At the time, black women workers in the North earned an average weekly salary of $10; their southern counterparts brought home less than $2 per week. Walker-trained women fared much better. "A diploma from Lelia College of Hair Culture is a Passport to Prosperity," assured one advertisement. In a 1913 letter to the company, Mrs. Williams James of Columbus, Ohio, said, "We have been able to purchase a home and overmeet our obligations. Before I started out as an agent in Madam Walker's employ, I made the regular working woman's wage, but at this writing I average $23 a week."

"Open your own shop. Secure prosperity and freedom. Many women of all ages, confronted with the problem of earning a livlihood have mastered the Walker System," read a typical Walker ad. In an era of wildly exaggerated advertising, the Walker claims were rather modest. They were also truthful. Almost any woman with drive, determination, and creativity could pass the Walker course, whether she took it by mail, at one of the Lelia Colleges in Pittsburgh, New York, or Indianapolis, or from Walker and her traveling instructors.

One of Walker's top representatives, Marjorie Stewart Joyner, credited her husband's mother with her success. Telling her story years later, Joyner said that as a recent graduate of a white beauty school, she had offered to shampoo and style her mother-in-law's hair. But Joyner's technique, learned on naturally straight Caucasian hair, failed to work on her relative's hair.

Instead of being angry, the elder Mrs. Joyner gave her daughter-in-law some advice. "She said she had heard of a black woman who was coming to Chicago to teach a course about our hair," Joyner recalled later. "And she gave me $17 to take the course."

Teaching that course was Madam C. J. Walker, who showed Joyner how to use a hot steel comb to dry and soften the hair. Joyner, who found the process "amazing," repaid Walker by demonstrating the "French marcel wave," a technique she had learned in the white beauty school. Impressed, Walker asked the young woman to join her company.

Joyner opened her own Walker beauty salon in Chicago; several years later, she became a recruiter and trainer of Walker agents and then national supervisor of the Lelia Colleges and all Walker Beauty Schools. With Joyner and others as instructors, the Walker company eventually opened a dozen beauty schools.

In late 1916, Walker began offering her courses to black colleges throughout the South. Many schools accepted her plan, which included the installation, without charge to the colleges, of campus beauty parlors and training centers. Mary McLeod Bethune responded enthusiastically to the proposal. "For the past four years my girls and myself have been using your Wonderful Hair Grower," she wrote Walker in March 1917. "We have proven it to be very beneficial indeed and would be glad to place it in [the Daytona Educational Industrial Training School] as a course of study."

Hairdressing and barbering had a long tradition in the American black community. In the days of slavery, black men and women often tended to their masters' hair. Centuries earlier in Africa, hairstyles, their versions as varied as the hundreds of tribes inhabiting the continent, had denoted marital status, age, and social status. African women spent hours,

Marjorie Stewart Joyner, trained in a white beauty school, botched the job when she tried to style her mother-in-law's hair. After she enrolled in Walker's classes, however, she became a master of her trade and opened her own Walker salon.

even days, creating intricate, beautiful braids into which they wove shells, beads, and other ornaments. Some women wore wigs made of human and animal hair or plant fibers; others dyed their hair with soot or colored it with red clay. Whatever they did with their hair, African women did proudly.

By the 20th century in America, slavery had severely damaged black pride. Although blacks managed to retain some vestiges of their African heritage in language, music, religion, and food, their white masters had forcibly eliminated many other traditions. Blackness had come to signify bondage; Negroid hair and features to suggest inferiority.

Many blacks harbored ambivalent feelings about themselves, an uneasy mixture of racial pride and self-hatred born of their unique experience of oppression. As scholar and activist W. E. B. Du Bois once put it: "One ever feels his two-ness—an American, a Negro; two souls, two thoughts, two unreconciled strivings; two warring ideals in one dark body."

Because of widespread racial mixing, many 20th-century American Negroes had European and Native American as well as African ancestry. Their multi-racial biological heritage reflected itself in the shade of their skin and the texture of their hair. It also left them with the tricky task of defining who they were in American society.

When it came to black women and their hair, the question seemed all the more loaded. A black woman might be proud of her heritage and, at the same time, eager to match the prevailing standards of "white" beauty. Acutely aware of the image debate, Walker sought to create a look that was truly Afro-American and that also addressed women's concerns about their appearance. Her solution: to urge women to concentrate on grooming and on emphasizing their own good points without trying to imitate whites.

"Right here let me correct the erroneous impression held by some that I claim to straighten the hair,"

she once told a reporter. "I want the great masses of
my people to take a greater pride in their personal
appearance and to give their hair proper attention. . . . And I dare say that in the next ten years it
will be a rare thing to see a kinky head of hair and it
will not be straight either."

Walker considered the ritual of her system as
important as any resulting hairstyle. She taught her
agents to create an atmosphere in which their customers would feel pampered and valued. The personal attention gave women a chance to focus on
themselves, boosting their confidence and self-esteem
in the process. For black women, who rarely found
themselves valued in American society, the psycho-
logical lift was enormous.

Walker agents learned a philosophy of inner and
outer beauty. "To be beautiful," asserted the Walker
Beauty School textbook, "does not refer alone to the
arrangement of the hair, the perfection of the com-
plexion or to the beauty of the form. . . . To be
beautiful, one must combine these qualities with a
beautiful mind and soul; a beautiful character. Phys-
ical and mental cleanliness, together with [good
health] are essential to attain loveliness."

Most manufacturers of black hair-care and cos-
metic products featured glamorous mulatto or ideal-
ized white women in their ads. Not Walker. She used
her own photograph on her products and in her
advertisements, allowing customers to see that she,
like many of them, was a black woman with decidedly
Negroid facial features. The ads seemed to say: Buy
Walker's products and look like Walker; look like
Walker, and you too may achieve her success.

Walker promoted that notion among her agents
as well as her customers. In one letter about literature
for her agents, she told her attorney, "In those
circulars I wish you would use the words 'our' and 'we'
instead of 'I' and 'my.' "

The Walker agents' handbook stressed the impor-

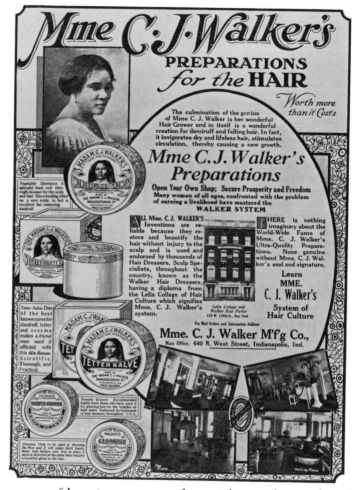

Walker's advertisements covered all bases. This one, which ran in The Messenger and other publications, includes the entrepreneur's photograph, pictures of her offices and salons, descriptions of her products, an invitation to become a Walker agent, a plug for the Lelia Colleges, and a block of hard-hitting copy: "All Mme. C. J. Walker's Inventions are reliable," asserts the ad.

tance of keeping accurate financial records, spotless beauty salons, and an impeccable appearance. "See that your hair always looks well . . . to interest others," the handbook counseled. Walker also encouraged her agents to be socially conscious community leaders, urging them to contribute part of their profits to charity.

Walker customers were encouraged to take treatments, but Walker knew that not all black women could afford them. "Do not be narrow and selfish to the extent that you would not sell goods to anyone because they do not take the treatment from you,"

Walker told her agents. "We are anxious to help all humanity, the poor as well as the rich, especially those of our race."

Genuinely interested in aiding other blacks, Walker also knew that her own well-publicized philanthropy increased sales. Every time she donated money to a black institution, she linked the purchase of Walker products with the well-being of black America.

Whenever she could, Walker spent her money in the black community. Constructing a group of houses for Indianapolis blacks in 1916, for example, she employed 50 black workers. "My business is largely supported by my own people, so why shouldn't I spend my money so that it will go back into colored homes?" she remarked to a reporter. "By giving my work to colored men they are thus able to employ others and if not directly, indirectly I am creating more jobs for our boys and girls."

As her agents increased in number and local influence, Walker decided to create a national organization for them. Modeled on some of the benevolent societies of the time, The Madam C. J. Walker Hair Culturists Union of America was designed to foster cooperation among the agents and to protect them from competitors who were imitating Walker products and selling inferior goods at lower prices.

In August 1917, more than 200 delegates met at Philadelphia's Union Baptist Church for the group's first national convention. The hall hummed with excitement as the women arrived, each probably wondering who would win the prize for most successful sales agent of the year. They were also eager to tell Walker how they were educating their children, purchasing homes, and contributing to the charities in their communities.

As Walker entered the assembly hall, all the well-coiffed heads turned in her direction. In her

Proudly wearing their membership badges (opposite page), delegates to the first annual convention of the Madam C. J. Walker Hair Culturists Union of America assemble in Philadelphia in 1917. Addressing her agents, Walker (front row, center) recommended an active approach to selling: "Hit often and hit hard," she urged. "Strike with all your might."

speech, "Women's Duty to Women," Walker praised her agents, then reminded them of their responsibility to use their own success to advance other women. "I want to show that Walker agents are doing more than making money for themselves," she said. She also gave them advice on selling, which she compared to a battle. "Hit often and hit hard," she said. "Strike with all your might."

Most of all, she urged the women to pursue their dreams as she had pursued her own. "Perseverance is my motto," she told them. "It laid the Atlantic cable. It gave us the telegraph, telephone, and wireless. It gave to the world an Abraham Lincoln, and to a race freedom. It gave to the Negro Booker T. Washington and Tuskegee Institute. It made Frederick Douglass the great orator that he was, and it gave to the race Paul Laurence Dunbar and to poetry a new song."

Pursuing her theme, Walker said, "If I have accomplished anything in life it is because I have been willing to work hard. I never yet started anything doubtingly, and I have always believed in keeping at things with a vim. There is no royal flower strewn road to success, and if there is I have not found it, for what success I have obtained is the result of many sleepless nights and real hard work."

That hard work was clearly paying off. A few months before the Philadelphia convention, F. B. Ransom had given Walker an optimistic annual financial report. "At the rate you are going," he wrote, "we have now but five years before you will be rated as a millionaire."

Reporters, fascinated by Walker's wealth, often asked her about her net worth. Replying to a query from a *New York Times* reporter in late 1916, she said, "Well, until recently it gave me great pleasure to tell . . . the amount of money I made yearly, thinking it would inspire my hearers. But I found that for so doing some looked upon me as a boastful person who wanted to blow my own horn. . . . I will say, however, that my business last year yielded me an annual income which runs into six figures and I'm going to try to eclipse my 1915 record this year."

A year later, Walker responded to another press inquiry by saying, "I am not a millionaire, but I hope to be someday, not for the money, but because I could do so much to help my race."

7

"WE SHOULD PROTEST"

❧

IN 1916, WHEN Walker arrived in Harlem, a wave of black southern migrants was reaching its peak in New York and other northern cities. Sparking the migration was the promise of good jobs and a better life.

Coming after two years of boll weevil invasions, the summer floods of 1915 had made intolerable living conditions even worse for poor southerners. Jobless, homeless, and hungry, many blacks were forced to look for work outside the region. World War I, which had begun to ravage Europe in 1914, drastically reduced the supply of European immigrants. To fill positions in northern factories, employment agents swept through the South, ready to hire anyone willing to work, black or white.

The hundreds of thousands of blacks who fled the South between 1915 and 1920 sought not only work but escape from lynchings and segregation. As the *Defender*, a black Chicago newspaper, put it, "To die from the bite of frost is far more glorious than at the hands of a mob."

Of all the northern cities, New York—specifically, Harlem, the cultural and intellectual

Walker, who loved cars, pilots a snappy electric coupé, a vehicle especially popular with women in the century's first two decades. At top speed, an electric car moved no faster than 30 miles per hour, but it traveled silently, operated easily, and could run for 35 to 50 miles on one battery charge.

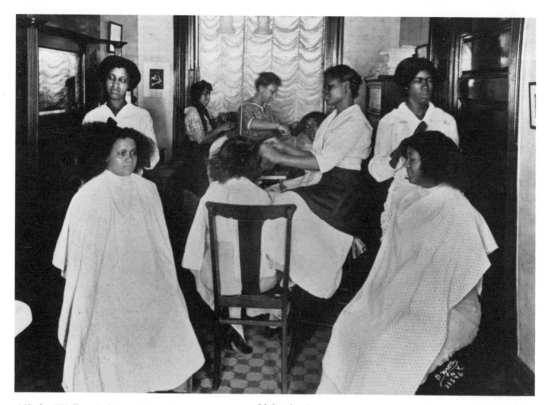

A'Lelia Walker Robinson (seated, front left) patronizes the beauty parlor of her namesake Lelia College in New York City. Among the busy salon's attendants is A'Lelia's daughter, Mae, who stands on the left side of the window at rear.

mecca of black America—exerted the strongest pull, not only on the southerners but on blacks across the nation. It was Harlem's residents who established trends in the black community; their tastes in music, books, art, and fashion influenced styles far beyond their city's borders.

In the realm of cosmetics and skin care, two recent European immigrants, Elizabeth Arden and Helena Rubenstein, dictated white fashion. For black women, the queen of beauty culture was a recent immigrant from Indianapolis, Madam C. J. Walker.

Walker's success mirrored the spirit of possibility many sensed in Harlem. Her elegant four-story, brick-and-limestone town house, which she shared with her daughter and granddaughter, quickly became a focal point for Harlem's elite. Harlemites vied for invitations to Walker's lavish dinner parties and musical evenings, which featured melodies played on her ceiling-high organ and on the gold-leafed harp and phonograph she had brought from Indianapolis.

Walker's 136th Street residence also housed Lelia College, which graduated 20 Walker hair culturists every 6 weeks. Also on the building's ground floor was the expansive Walker Hair Parlor; here, black women from all over Manhattan and Brooklyn experienced the Walker Method of hair care as they sipped tea and coffee in the calm, pearl gray surroundings. Helping Walker train the students and manage the salon were her daughter and granddaughter, Mae.

As Mae's 19th birthday approached, her mother and grandmother decided it was time to broaden her education and prepare her to take on more responsibility in the Walker company. In September 1916, A'Lelia enrolled Mae in Spelman Seminary in Atlanta, Georgia, the nation's first college for black women.

Meanwhile, the family business continued to prosper. In October, Walker factory shipping clerk Raymond Turner wrote his boss from Indianapolis: "We have more mail than anyone at the post office. . . . Miss Kelly sent a big shipping order to Mrs. Robinson of 13,234 Grower, 3,904 Glossine and 1,002 shampoos." In Pittsburgh alone, the Walker operation was bringing in $2,000 a week from sales of such popular products as Wonderful Hair Grower and Vegetable Shampoo.

The company's energetic chief executive had continued to act as its principal sales agent, traveling from state to state, making speeches, organizing demonstrations, and taking product orders. By the fall of 1916, however, the 48-year-old Walker was ready to turn some of this exhausting travel over to others; she knew she could count on Alice Kelly, former schoolteacher Alice Burnette, and her other handpicked, carefully trained executives to do the job. Departing on a swing through the South in September, Walker declared it would be her last.

From each stop, Walker sent a report back to headquarters. After visiting Salisbury, North Carolina, for example, she wrote happily, "I was very much flattered at the splendid turnout to hear my lecture. Both black and white came. They were all loud in their praise." In a note from Savannah, Georgia, she said, "My trip here was a howling success in that I have been able to get before thousands of people and all the big guns have shown me the greatest courtesies and kindness." And from Mississippi, she wrote, "I surely made a hit in Natchez and am sure we'll get some good business from there."

When Walker reached Washington, Georgia, she found the city in the midst of a disappointing cotton-harvesting season and consequent hard economic times. "I'm having quite a deal of success here with the work," she wrote, "but I've found so many poor people who cannot raise $25.00 that I've decided to let them have the trade for $10.00. . . . I put them on their honor to pay whenever they can."

From Georgia, Walker went on to the towns of her childhood. "Delta was honored Sunday," reported the local paper, "by a visit of the richest negro woman in the world, [Madam] C. J. Walker. . . . The visitor was very quiet and unassuming and a fine example to her race." In Delta, Walker received a warm welcome from Anna Burney Long, owner of the plantation where Walker had been born and the great-granddaughter of the man who had owned Walker's parents, Minerva and Owen Breedlove. After chatting with Long, Walker walked down the muddy road to the cabin where she and her family had lived.

She stood outside, remembering her parents, remembering her childhood. No one, she reflected, could have dreamed that little Sarah Breedlove would grow up to be the wealthiest black woman in America. Recalling the moment, Walker said she could not help but enjoy a sense of deep satisfaction and triumph.

Still, something was bothering her. All her life, she had possessed boundless energy, enabling her to help both herself and other people. Lately, however, she had noticed an occasional overwhelming sense of fatigue: Although her spirit was always willing, sometimes her body was not. Walker's doctor had warned her of high blood pressure, chiding her about her high-fat diet and her frantic pace, but she had found it almost impossible to slow down.

Then, traveling through Clarksdale, Mississippi, in mid-November, she was reminded of her own mortality. She wrote to Ransom about the event: "After leaving the church, we had to cross a railroad track. As soon as the car we were in got on the track we heard a man yelling, 'Get out of the way!' We looked around in time to see a freight train backing down on us, not a bell ringing or anything. The chauffeur in the nick of time put on more gas and shot forward. The train all but grazed the back of the car in which we were riding. I haven't been myself since."

The doctor who examined Walker after the near catastrophe advised her to take a long vacation. "I think instead of coming home, I will go to Hot Springs where I can really get rest and quietude," she wrote Ransom. "The doctor advises me to take not less than six weeks rest." At the bottom of Walker's letter, her traveling companion typed a postscript: "Dear Mr. Ransom," it said, "Thank goodness we have finally persuaded Mme. Walker to take that much needed rest. Today the doctor told me she was on the verge of a nervous breakdown. . . . You keep telling her after she gets to Hot Springs to remain there for the six weeks."

Mae Walker Robinson takes a break between classes at Spelman Seminary, the Atlanta, Georgia, college she entered in 1916. Known since 1924 as Spelman College, the school—the first U.S. institution of higher education for black women—was founded in 1881 as the Atlanta Baptist Female Seminary.

Walker obediently settled into a health spa in Hot Springs, Arkansas, but she still found it hard to relax. Within days of her arrival, she wrote to Ransom again: "I promise you I am going to let all business alone and look strictly after my health except little things which I am going to write to you about now. Ha. Ha."

Situated on the edge of central Arkansas's Ouachita National Forest, Hot Springs featured dozens of wells bubbling with steaming, mineral-laden water that was said to cure a variety of ailments. Wealthy visitors from all over the United States "took the waters" at Hot Springs and relaxed in the area's elegant, European-style bathhouses. The tense, over-tired Walker, her associates thought, was in the right place to relax—if she could manage to sit still for a few weeks.

Hoping to keep her at Hot Springs, Walker's daughter and Alice Kelly joined her there for the Christmas holidays. The three women spent much of their time at the luxurious bathhouse owned by the Knights of Pythias, a black fraternal organization. Every morning, Walker soaked herself in hot mineral water as she sipped a soothing herbal tea, then showered in a spray of brisk water jets. Afterward, wrapped in hot towels, she rested in a darkened room. Completing the regimen was a massage with fragrant oil.

Surprising her family and friends, Walker stayed at Hot Springs until February. Then, full of renewed energy, her promise to quit the road forgotten, she set off on a two-month trip through Texas and Louisiana. Along with her returned health came a surge of record-breaking business.

In April 1917, soon after Walker returned to New York, the United States entered World War I. The conflict triggered a debate in Harlem and throughout black America: Should black men enlist to fight? Many said yes, sure that their country would reward their loyalty with respect. Others, however, put civil rights before world war; they believed their country should grant them full rights as citizens before asking them to risk their life.

This group had very real reason for concern. Many whites felt threatened by blacks' increasingly outspoken stance and by their abandonment of the moderate approach of Booker T. Washington and his followers. On the rise since the end of the post–Civil War Reconstruction period, racism had reached terrifying proportions by the beginning of the 20th century's second decade.

The 1912 election of Democratic president Woodrow Wilson reversed much of the progress blacks had made after the Civil War. Campaigning for office, Wilson had promised black leaders that he would treat members of their race with "absolute fairness," that he would encourage their employment in federal agencies, and that he would establish a National Race Commission to study the health, education, and economic status of blacks.

After his election, Wilson—the first southerner to occupy the White House since the Civil War—reintroduced racial segregation in the nation's capital, forced many blacks from their federal jobs, and backed away from the Race Commission project.

By the beginning of Wilson's second term, the antiblack backlash was in full force. Zealously spurring it on was the Ku Klux Klan, the secret organization founded after the Civil War to reestablish white supremacy in the South. Klan "Knights" roamed the countryside, burning fiery crosses, kidnapping, flogging, and murdering minority citizens, especially blacks. Inspired by these hooded night riders, American racists embarked on an orgy of lynchings: Between 1885 and 1916, nearly 3,000 blacks met violent death at the hands of white mobs.

Despite such horrors, despite social and economic inequality, and despite the federal government's lack

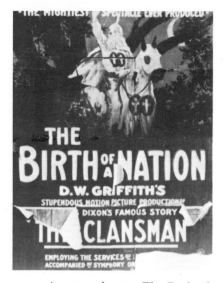

A poster advertises The Birth of a Nation, *an immensely popular 1915 movie that portrayed blacks as docile servants, corrupt politicians, or bloodthirsty rapists. Despite its historical inaccuracy and blatant sensationalism, the film reinforced some whites' belief that blacks deserved few political and economic rights.*

of interest in its black constituents, a number of prominent black leaders believed that members of their race should cooperate in the nation's war effort. Such a demonstration of loyalty, they believed, would prove to whites that blacks had an equal stake in the nation's welfare and therefore deserved equal rights as citizens.

Among this group of committed people were two leaders of the National Association for the Advancement of Colored People (NAACP): W. E. B. Du Bois, editor of the NAACP magazine, *The Crisis*, and NAACP field secretary James Weldon Johnson. Both men advised blacks to "close ranks" with white America in support of the war effort.

Strongly approving the Du Bois–Johnson approach, Walker lent her name—by now widely known in both the black and the white communities—to the government's black-recruitment effort. She threw herself into the cause with her usual enthusiasm. Visiting training camps around the country, she offered moral support and encouraged young black enlisted men to become outstanding soldiers.

After Walker's visit to his post, one sergeant wrote her a letter. "We all remember you," he said. "We have often spoken of you and of the words of consolation which you gave us at Camp Sherman, Ohio, on the eve of our departure. Those words have stayed with the boys longer than any spoken by anyone that I have known or heard of."

Then, in the summer of 1917, major race riots swept several American cities. The worst of these bloody uprisings took place in East St. Louis, Illinois, where mobs murdered 39 blacks, seriously injured hundreds of others, and drove thousands of families from their homes. In some cases, whites torched the homes of blacks, then shot them as they tried to escape. As assailants drowned, burned, and beat black children, women, and men, white policemen either watched calmly or helped the mobs.

After the riot, a profound sense of outrage united the nation's blacks. Adding to their anger and grief was the knowledge that thousands of young black men had demonstrated their support for America by joining the armed forces—knowledge particularly galling to those who, like Walker, had endorsed enlistment. In Harlem, Walker joined other leading citizens to design a way to express the community's pain and to demand an end to unchecked mob violence. The result: the Negro Silent Protest Parade, staged in Manhattan on July 28, 1917.

Shortly after noon on that Saturday, some 10,000 black New Yorkers began a somber, purposeful march down Fifth Avenue. Block after block, no sound broke the city's hush but the dirgelike roll of muffled drums and the muted thunder of marching feet. More than 20,000 spectators, silent as the marchers, lined the avenue.

In the parade, dark-suited men carried banners and signs protesting Jim Crow laws, mob violence, and disfranchisement. Treat Us so That We May Love Our Country, read one banner. The female marchers, who included a number of Walker agents, wore white dresses and escorted rows of neatly dressed children.

Heartened by the public show of solidarity, Walker and her colleagues pressed on, hoping they could persuade national officials to make lynching a federal crime. (Like murder—which it was—lynching was a state, rather than a federal crime; because the southern states where it was most often committed almost never prosecuted lynchers, civil libertarians hoped for a special federal law banning the barbaric practice.)

The Harlem group composed a petition, then requested a meeting with President Wilson to discuss

Marchers fill Manhattan's Fifth Avenue during the Negro Silent Protest Parade in 1917. Sparked by a murderous attack on blacks in East St. Louis, Illinois, and organized by Walker and her associates, the parade drew 10,000 participants and twice as many spectators.

the issue. Along with Walker, James Weldon Johnson, and W. E. B. Du Bois, the petition signers included the Reverend Adam Clayton Powell, Sr., of Harlem's Abyssinian Baptist Church; Harlem realtor John E. Nail; and *New York Age* publisher Fred Moore. Although the petition was low-keyed and courteous in tone, it made its point unmistakably clear.

"Mobs have harried and murdered colored citizens time and time again with impunity, culminating in the latest atrocity at East St. Louis," said the text in part. "We believe that this spirit of lawlessness is doing untold injury to our country. . . . We ask, therefore, that lynching and mob violence be made a national crime punishable by the laws of the United States."

In response to the Harlem delegates' request, Wilson's secretary, Joseph Tumulty, promised them an appointment with the president. On August 1, four days after the Silent Parade, Walker and her friends presented themselves at the White House with their petition. As scheduled, Tumulty appeared in the executive waiting room at exactly 12 o'clock. He greeted the group cordially—then said the president was busy signing a bill dealing with farm animal feed. Wilson, Tumulty said, would be unable to see the black petitioners.

Walker and her friends had not come to Washington expecting miracles. They knew Wilson's views on racial matters reflected the Old South; they knew he had abandoned the projected Race Commission; they knew of the remark he had made to a group of black leaders in 1913: "Segregation is not humiliating but a benefit, and ought to be so regarded by you gentlemen." Still, the Harlemites had hoped the president would understand the urgency of their message, and that he would keep his appointment with them. Vastly disappointed, they presented their petition to Tumulty and left the White House.

The group went on to visit several senators and congressmen to ask for their support. Congress eventually appointed a committee to investigate the East St. Louis riot. Its members also introduced two new antilynching bills; like all the others, however, they met defeat at the hands of southern legislators.

Despite the government's failure to move against lynching, Walker believed there might be political leverage in staying involved, and she continued to urge blacks to support the war effort. Addressing a convention of Walker agents in August 1917, she advised her listeners "to remain loyal to our homes, our country and our flag." At the same time, however, she maintained that blacks should keep on fighting for justice and equal rights.

"This is the greatest country under the sun," she said. "But we must not let our love of country, our patriotic loyalty cause us to abate one whit in our

Walker admired newspaperwoman Ida Wells-Barnett, and the fiery antilynching activist returned the feeling. "To see her phenomenal rise," said Wells-Barnett of Walker, "made me take pride anew in Negro womanhood."

protest against wrong and injustice. We should protest until the American sense of justice is so aroused that such affairs as the East St. Louis riot be forever impossible."

Just as Walker had encouraged her agents to become community leaders, she now encouraged them to become political lobbyists (individuals who try to influence lawmakers on behalf of special-interest groups). After listening to Walker's 1917 speech, the agents voted to send a telegram to Wilson:

> Honored Sir: . . . Knowing that no people in all the world are more loyal and patriotic than the Colored people of America, we respectfully submit to you this our protest against the continuation of such wrongs and injustices [as the East St. Louis race riot] and we further respectfully urge that you as President of these United States use your great influence that congress enact the necessary laws to prevent a recurrence of such disgraceful affairs.

(A year later, Wilson finally issued a public statement about lynching. The president, reported the *New York Times* on July 27, 1918, denounced "mob spirit and mob action as emulating German lawlessness," and urged the country's governors, law officers, and citizens to "actively and watchfully" bring an end to lynching. His mild words, followed up by no specific proposals for controlling lynching, had no apparent effect on the ongoing violence against blacks.)

Realizing that her wealth and high visibility made people listen to what she said, Walker became increasingly outspoken on political issues. Sometimes, her self-confidence led her to take militant stands avoided by her more cautious associates. She surprised many of them, for example, by advertising in *The Messenger*, a socialist newspaper published by future labor leader A. Philip Randolph.

Randolph made no secret of his distaste for Walker's "frivolous" society parties, but he also publicly praised her political and economic efforts for blacks. He had good reason to respect Walker's achievements as a businesswoman: *The Messenger* was largely funded by income from a beauty salon owned by his wife, Lucille Green, a close friend of Walker's and one of the first graduates of Walker's Lelia College in New York.

Deeply involved in her business and increasingly committed to political activities, Walker still found time to plan and build her dream house. In late 1916, she had bought a large piece of land in Irvington-on-Hudson, a wealthy community just north of New York City. Her purchase of the property, perched on the eastern bank of the broad Hudson River, had originally raised eyebrows among Irvington's white residents.

"On her first visits to inspect her property," reported the *New York Times*, "the villagers, noting her color, were frankly puzzled, but when it became known that she was the owner . . . they could only gasp in astonishment. 'Impossible!' they exclaimed. 'No woman of her race could own such a place.' To say that the village, when the report was verified, was surprised, would be putting the case mildly. 'Does she really intend to live there, or is she building it as a speculation?' the people asked."

The *Defender*, on the other hand, regarded the situation with some amusement. Walker's purchase of the Irvington estate, said the black newspaper, had "created a furore, for one of the Race was invading the sacred domains of New York's most sacred aristocracy."

Happily looking forward to her new home with its panoramic views of the river and the towering New Jersey Palisades, Walker paid no attention to the controversy. And, as things turned out, her neigh-

The New York Times

Wealthiest Negro Woman's Suburban Mansion

Estate at Irvington, Overlooking Hudson and Containing All the Attractions That a Big Fortune Commands

To own a country estate on the banks of the Hudson has been the dream of many a New Yorker. It is a dream come true in the case of Mrs. Sarah J Walker. the city's wealthiest negro woman. Mrs. Walker, or Mme. Walker, as she is more generally known, has built a $250,000 home at Irvington. Twelve years ago she was a washerwoman, glad of a chance to do any one's family wash for $1.50 a day. Her friends now acclaim her the Hetty Green of her race. They say she has a cool million, or nearly that.

Ground for the Walker dwelling was broken eight months ago, and a large gang of workmen have been kept busy ever since. Although the house is nearly completed, it will not be ready for occupancy for several months. When it is finished it is to be one of the show places on the Hudson. Of late Mme. Walker, in her high-powered motor car, has been a familiar visitor in Irvington. On her first visits to inspect her property the villagers, noting her color, were frankly puzzled. Later, when it became known that she was the owner of the pretentious dwelling, they could only gasp in astonishment.

"Impossible!" they exclaimed. "No

red tile, is in the Italian renaissance style of architecture, and was designed by V. W. Tandy, a negro architect. It is 113 feet long, 60 wide, and stands in the centre of a four-and-a-quarter-acre plot. It is fireproof, of structural tile with an outer covering of cream-colored stucco, and has thirty-four rooms. In the basement are a gymnasium, baths and showers, kitchen and pantry, servants' dining room, power room for an organ, and storage vaults for valuables.

The main entrance is on the north side. The visitor enters a marble room, whence a marble stairway leads to the floor above. On the first floor are the library and conservatory, a living room

maids of all work. In addition to these she has a social secretary and a nurse. On the third floor are also bathrooms, a billiard room, and a children's nursery. Mme. Walker loves children. They are frequent guests at her home. She provides toys for them, likes to see them at play, and does what she can to make them happy.

Plans for furnishing the house call for a degree of elegance and extravagance that a princess might envy There are to be bronze and marble statuary, sparkling cut glass candelabra, paintings, rich tapestries, and countless other things which will make the place a wonder house.

the South, and New England. She is content to let her chauffeur drive the big cars. She has, however, a small electric coupé which she drives herself on shopping tours.

Mme. Walker is preparing to entertain her friends on a large scale in the new house. She will have as her companion most of the time her daughter, Mrs. Lelia Walker Robinson, associated with her in business.

"I was born forty-nine years ago," she said in speaking of her life. "was married at 14, and was left a widow at 20 with a little girl to support. If I have accomplished anything in life it is because I have been willing to work hard. I never yet started anything doubtingly, and I have always believed in keeping at things with a vim. When, a little more than twelve years ago, I was a washerwoman, I was considered a good washerwoman and laundress. I am proud of that fact. At times I also did cooking, but, work as I would, I seldom could make more than $1.50 a day. I got my start by giving myself a start.' It is often the best way. I believe in push, and we must push ourselves.

"I was at my tubs one morning with a heavy wash

Irvington Home of Wealthy Negro Woman, Now Nearing Completion.   Brown Bros.

21 by 32 feet, furnished in Italian style,   On the side of the house facing the   before me. As I bent over the wash-

---

By 1917, Walker was news, even in the white press. Reporting on her mansion, the New York Times noted that it was "in the most exclusive part of Irvington Village." Of Walker, the paper said, "Twelve years ago she was a washerwoman, glad of a chance to do any one's family wash for $1.50 a day. Her friends now . . . say she has a cool million, or nearly that."

bors' chilly attitude thawed soon after she moved in. "Mme. Walker's unassuming ways kept down any possible friction that might have arisen due to her presence," one observer noted later. "Instead of dislike, her neighbors have learned to respect her."

The new house was nearing completion in September 1917, when Walker attended the 10th annual convention of the National Equal Rights League in Manhattan. At the meeting, she met an old acquaintance, journalist and antilynching crusader Ida B. Wells-Barnett. The businesswoman and the activist had first met several years earlier, just as Walker was starting her business.

"I was one of the skeptics that paid little heed to her predictions as to what she was going to do," Wells-Barnett recalled years later. "To see her phenomenal rise made me take pride anew in Negro womanhood."

After hosting a banquet for the convention's officers, Walker invited Wells-Barnett to visit with her and to inspect her new house. The visitor appeared properly impressed with the sunken Italian garden, the swimming pool, and the sweeping terraces, but she wondered about the size of the place. "I asked her on one occasion what on earth she would do with a thirty room house," Wells-Barnett noted in her autobiography. "She said, 'I want plenty of room in which to entertain my friends. I have worked so hard all my life that I would like to rest.' "

Rest, of course, was exactly what Walker usually managed to avoid. Several weeks after Wells-Barnett's visit, the entrepreneur's blood pressure shot up, and her physician sent her to a medical clinic in Battle Creek, Michigan. There, doctors made an announcement she did not want to hear: If she had any interest in remaining alive, she "must give little or no attention again to business or heavy social activities." ◖◗

8

RACE WOMAN

NO MATTER WHAT her doctors said, Walker could not—or would not—slow down her hectic pace. Within a week of her release from the Battle Creek clinic, she traveled to Des Moines, Iowa, to speak at an NAACP fund-raising banquet.

Walker put up a good front, but George Woodson, the local attorney who introduced her to the audience in Des Moines, realized she was not in the best of health. "The eloquent force which she put into that speech in spite of her nervous state, greatly alarmed me," he wrote to F. B. Ransom. "I took her pulse in the reception room after the meeting and tried to get her away from the great mass of common people who crowded about her to admire and compliment her. But it was no use. She loved those common people and just would not leave them."

Walker thrived on the knowledge that her success could inspire and help other black Americans. She also thrilled to the enthusiasm she inspired in her audiences. From Des Moines, she embarked on a string of appearances designed to raise money for the NAACP. "I had a crowded house and applause all through the lecture," she wrote Ransom from Chi-

Walker—uncharacteristically—relaxes at home. Despite frequent warnings from her doctor, the dynamic entrepreneur found it hard to take it easy: "I promise you I am going to let all business alone and look strictly after my health," she once wrote attorney F. B. Ransom. Then she added, "Ha. Ha."

cago. "I would have to wait for them three minutes to get quiet before I could begin again." She went from Chicago to Indianapolis, then to Columbus, Ohio, and Pittsburgh. "I have packed houses everywhere I have gone, notwithstanding the downpour snow," she noted happily.

Meanwhile, Walker's "dream of dreams," her new home in Irvington, was almost ready for occupancy. By the late spring of 1918, she had finished most of the decorating, sparing no expense in her effort to create a breathtaking environment for herself, her daughter, and her granddaughter.

Walker lined the walls of the elegant main hall with handmade tapestries and filled the hall's cabinets with bronze and ivory statuettes collected from her travels. In the dining room, she installed handpainted ceilings and recessed lighting to create a fairy-tale atmosphere for her dinner guests. She stocked the paneled library with works by great American authors from Paul Laurence Dunbar to Mark Twain, along with rare books from all over the world.

The drawing room contained not only a grand piano trimmed in 24-carat gold leaf but an organ whose music was piped through the entire house. From the first floor, a broad, curved marble staircase led to the lavish bedrooms above. Gazing from the windows of her own chamber, furnished with a four-poster bed canopied in red velvet, Walker could see the New Jersey Palisades across the river. The view was slightly reminiscent of the Vicksburg bluffs of her youth, but light-years from her present circumstances.

Breathlessly reporting on what it called Walker's "wonder house," the *New York Times* credited it with "a degree of elegance and extravagance that a princess might envy." After describing the interior and the gardens, the paper noted that "the garage [has] apartments for the chauffeur and gardener. Mme.

Walker maintains four automobiles. . . . She is content to let her chauffeur drive the big cars. She has, however, a small electric coupé, which she drives herself on shopping tours."

Soon after the Walker women moved into their luxurious residence in June 1918, they entertained Enrico Caruso, the era's most celebrated opera star. Learning that the Walkers had not yet named their new home, Caruso made a suggestion: The place, he said, reminded him of the grand estates of his homeland, Italy; why not use letters from A'Lelia's name—LElia WAlker RObinson—and call it a villa? The idea appealed to his hostesses, who thereupon christened the magnificent house Villa Lewaro.

Walker took immense pleasure in the villa, a place "that only Negro money had bought." She once said she thought of her home as a black institution, a monument that would "convince members of [my] race of the wealth of business possibilities within the race, to point to young Negroes what a lone woman accomplished and to inspire them to do big things."

To help look after her villa, Walker sent for the butler and housekeeper, Mr. and Mrs. Bell, she had employed in Indianapolis. As soon as the couple arrived, Walker went to work in her garden, labor that she found extremely relaxing. Writing to a friend later that summer, she said, "Every morning at six o'clock I am at work in the garden, pulling weeds, gathering berries and vegetables. [You] should see me now . . . all dressed up in overalls. . . . I am a full-fledged 'farmerette.' We are putting up fruit and vegetables by the wholesale."

Calmly planting seedlings and pruning rosebushes, Walker seemed to be following her doctor's orders at last. But in midsummer, she received a tempting invitation from the National Association of Colored Women. Walker had been the main contributor to the NACW drive to pay off the mortgage

Ransom exchanged hundreds of letters with Walker over the years. Even though the two had become close friends, their correspondence retained a formal tone: Walker addressed the attorney as "Mr. Ransom" and signed her mail "Yours respectfully, Mme. C. J. Walker." Ransom, in turn, always wrote to "Dear Madam."

on the home of black abolitionist Frederick Douglass; now the NACW proposed to honor her at its annual convention. The meeting would be held in Denver, the city where Walker had started her business 13 years earlier. Delighted, she promised to attend.

Walker, who had made the largest individual contribution ($500) to the Douglass fund, played a key role in the mortgage-burning ceremony. As the audience sang "Hallelujah, 'Tis Done," NACW president Mary B. Talbert held the mortgage document as Walker touched a burning candle to its edge. Watching the paper crumble to ashes, the crowd rose to its feet with a storm of applause.

A few weeks after the convention, the National Negro Business League honored Walker and Vertner W. Tandy, the architect who had designed both her Manhattan town house and her suburban villa. Tandy, New York State's first certified black architect, had attended Tuskegee Institute, where Booker T. Washington had encouraged him to study architecture. By 1917, when he began designing Walker's home, Tandy had already completed many schools, churches, and private residences. Addressing the NNBL audience, he said, "There is one person who has contributed more to architecture for Negroes than any person or group of persons in this country and that person is . . . Madam C. J. Walker."

As Walker thanked him, she was probably thinking of the house party she had scheduled for late August. Guest of honor at the weekend celebration was to be Emmett J. Scott, former private secretary to Booker T. Washington and a principal founder of the NNBL. Walker had planned her party as a tribute to Scott's recent appointment to an important government post: special assistant to the secretary of war in charge of Negro affairs.

Walker's guest list read like a copy of *Who's Who in Black America*. Invited to the gala were leading black Baptist and Methodist ministers, educators

Dean William Pickens of Morgan College and Charlotte Hawkins Brown, founder of Palmer Memorial Institute; political activists Ida B. Wells-Barnett and A. Philip Randolph; newspaper publishers Fred Moore of the *New York Age* and Robert Sengstacke Abbott of the *Chicago Defender.*

Also asked to the celebration were several white NAACP members, including board chairman Joel Spingarn; president Moorfield Storey; secretary Mary White Ovington; and vice-president and treasurer Oswald Garrison Villard, editor of the *New York Evening Post.*

Others invitees included bibliophile Arthur Schomburg; Jesse Moorland, senior secretary of the YMCA's Colored Men's Department; banker Maggie Lena Walker; AME bishop and NAACP board vice-president John Hurst; NAACP assistant secretary Walter White; NAACP field secretary James Weldon Johnson and his brother, composer J. Rosamond Johnson; physician and former minister to Haiti Henry Watson Furniss; composer and concert singer Harry T. Burleigh; Margaret Murray Washington; poet William Stanley Braithwaite; and Carter G. Woodson, founder of the Association for the Study of Negro Life and History.

The Villa Lewaro weekend proved an immense success. Writing to Walker later, Emmett Scott said, "It will be a very great pleasure during all the years to come that we were the first official guests entertained at Villa Lewaro. The wonderful gathering of friends . . . was beyond compare. No such assemblage has ever gathered at the private home of any representative of our race, I am sure."

The party had included more than good food and lighthearted conversation; guests had also talked of such serious matters as the situation of black soldiers in Europe. Everyone had heard the frontline reports about heroic actions by black troops, particularly those of Harlem's own 369th Regiment. Popularly

Workmen put the finishing touches on Villa Lewaro, Walker's opulent mansion on the east bank of New York's Hudson River. The estate's title, suggested by a visiting Italian opera singer, derived from the name of Walker's daughter, LElia WAlker RObinson.

A'Lelia Robinson pauses in the drawing room at Villa Lewaro. Although she appreciated the comfort and beauty of her mother's mansion, A'Lelia found life in Irvington too staid; she preferred the bright lights and lively parties of Harlem.

known as the Hell Fighters, the 369th had been in ongoing combat for longer than any other American regiment and had been the first Allied unit to reach Germany's Rhine River.

Everyone had also heard reports of widespread racism within the military. Walker and her friends were beginning to wonder how black soldiers would fare when they returned to the United States. Would the nation reward their heroic efforts with new respect? Or would white America continue to treat these men as second-class citizens? The group at Lewaro resolved to fight for the rights of returning black veterans.

As the war dragged on into 1918, the Walker women became increasingly involved in the civilian war effort. Madam Walker promoted the sale of war bonds in the black community and joined the advisory board of the Motor Corps of America, a war-relief support effort. A'Lelia drove an ambulance for the Motor Corps, helping to transport wounded black returnees. She also worked with the Circle for Negroes' War Relief, supervising the making of bandages and other first-aid supplies.

The war finally ended in Allied victory on November 11, 1918. Like the rest of the nation, Walker rejoiced, celebrating with friends in Boston and sending all her employees home for the day. The following month, she accepted an invitation from Mayor John F. Hylan of New York to help the city welcome the troops home from Europe.

As Christmas approached, Walker went into her usual preholiday whirl, ordering festive meals, decorating her house, and choosing gifts for her family, friends, and employees. On December 23, her 51st birthday, mountains of Christmas cards competed for space with an avalanche of birthday greetings from friends and admiring strangers.

Walker's holiday guests began arriving on the afternoon of Christmas Eve. One of her best friends,

Hallie Queen, later wrote a description of the next few days:

Christmas Eve was spent most happily with music and song. Madame retired early as she usually did. At twelve o'clock, however, she awakened everyone who had gone to bed to wish him a "Merry Christmas."

Early Christmas morning, when we returned to the house [after church], we found Madame waiting for us before a glowing fireplace. Christmas greetings and gifts were exchanged and enjoyed until breakfast time.

It was significant that in that beautiful state dining room, with its wonderful furnishings and rich indirect lighting and all the material good that life could expect, Madame insisted upon our kneeling while she returned to God thanks for the gift of the Christ child and for all other gifts that had come to her. The theme of her prayer was humility and awe in the presence of God.

First, there was a distinguished minister, Rev. Brooks of Baltimore, who charmed us with stories of his European travels; then Mrs. [May Howard] Jackson, the brilliant moulder [sculptor] of human faces; her husband, W. T. S. Jackson, the mathematician; Lieut. O. Simmons, the army officer; a wounded overseas soldier wearing a *croix de guerre* [a French medal for heroism] and a sailor from a recently torpedoed vessel; Mr. Williams, the politician; Mr. [Lloyd] Thomas, one of Madame's secretaries; Mrs. [Agnes] Prosser, her sister-in-law; and I who had no claim to greatness other than that I was her friend.

After dinner we went into the wonderful music room and listened to old Christmas carols or read in the library from the magnificent selection of books owned by Mme. Walker.

Christmas night we motored in to New York City to attend a basketball game at the Manhattan Casino. Mme's entrance was the signal for an ovation and she was at once requested to throw the ball from her box.

The following day was to be a great day for she had been invited by the Mayor of the City to go out on his boat and observe the return of the Atlantic Fleet.

So ended . . . Christmas . . . and it was impressed upon my mind a memory of her goodness, devotion, reverence, humility and faith. ❧

9

THE LEGACY

B Y JANUARY 1919, the Madam C. J. Walker
Manufacturing Company had become black America's most successful business. Sales for 1918 had
topped a quarter of a million dollars; with the
introduction of five new products in 1919, Walker's
accountants expected the company's income to rise
still further.

Walker's financial health was booming, but her
personal health was not. In early 1919, her doctor,
Colonel Joseph Ward, put his foot down: It would be
nothing less than suicide, he said, if a woman with
her soaring blood pressure maintained a day-to-day
involvement with business. Walker must leave her
company in the capable hands of her attorney, her
agents, and her sales representatives.

Reluctantly, Walker obeyed Ward's orders—up
to a point. She continued to stay in regular contact
with her main office, and to direct corporate development and long-range sales strategy. She also
started spending more time on political activity.

During the recently ended war, Walker had
concluded that if black Americans were to attain

*Walker (second row, second from the left) reunites with a group
of old friends outside the Indianapolis YMCA, the building she had
helped endow in 1913. Standing in the first row (second from the
left) is George Knox, the newspaper publisher who persuaded
Walker to settle in the Indiana city in 1910; fourth from the right
in the back row is Robert Lee Brokenburr, the attorney who joined
Walker's company during its early days in the Midwest.*

97

their full rights as citizens, they would have to assert themselves in all aspects of national and international affairs. After the war, she paid careful attention to the peace negotiations, conducted in Paris between defeated Germany and the victorious Allied nations: the United States, Great Britain, France, Italy, Japan, and 23 other powers.

Walker and many of her colleagues feared that the peace treaty negotiators would ignore the rights of both black Americans and blacks in Europe's African colonies. Hoping to influence the treaty makers, several black leaders—W. E. B. Du Bois and William Monroe Trotter among them—decided to hold their own Paris meetings. Du Bois organized a group called the Pan-African Congress; Trotter, who had already founded the National Equal Rights League (NERL), held a meeting to elect delegates to his own alternative Paris peace conference. Among those selected as representatives were Walker and her friend Ida Wells-Barnett.

Walker's association with NERL alarmed her chief of operations. "You must always bear in mind that you have a large business, whereas the others who are going have nothing," Ransom lectured his boss. "There are many ways in which your business can be circumscribed and hampered," he added, "so as to practically put you out of business." In other words, Ransom, who considered NERL a radical, possibly even subversive organization, feared that Walker's connection with it could turn people against both her and her products.

NERL, which campaigned for integration and social justice, might have served as a model for the civil rights organizations of the 1960s. Although its demands seem moderate today, some cautious blacks did indeed regard it as dangerous. Walker, however, mapped her own path as usual. She valued Ransom's judgment, but she did not always agree with him and sometimes ignored his advice.

Home from the war, a wounded member of the Harlem Hell Fighters greets a Manhattan well-wisher in 1919. Although she was apprehensive about the future of the nation's black veterans, Walker was sure of one thing: "They will come back," she said, "to face like men whatever is in store for them and like men defend themselves, their families, and their homes."

Trotter, denied a passport by the State Department, never managed to field a Paris delegation. Du Bois, who did convene his Pan-African Congress in the French capital, presented his delegates' resolutions to members of the official peace conference, but to no avail. The Treaty of Versailles, signed in June 1919, would contain no guarantees of equality or self-determination for the world's people of color.

Disappointed but not discouraged, Walker continued to speak out for her race. She was particularly emphatic about the debt America owed its black veterans. Her strong stand on the issue brought sharp criticism from Colonel William Jay Schieffelin, the white treasurer of the Welfare League of an all-black infantry unit. Schieffelin, who believed blacks should

Walker, representing the International League of Darker Peoples (ILDP), attends a 1919 New York City conference with S. Kuroiwa (center), Japan's delegate to the Versailles Peace Conference. ILDP members, who also included future labor leader A. Phillip Randolph and Harlem clergyman Adam Clayton Powell, Sr., hoped to ensure the postwar rights of nonwhites through an alliance with the Japanese and other non-European peoples. Their efforts failed; the Treaty of Versailles included no special provisions for people of color.

take a very soft approach to the rights question, told Walker that her strident demands would do more harm than good. Walker, being Walker, refused to back down one inch.

"Their country called them to defend its honor on the battlefield of Europe," she told Schieffelin, "and they have bravely, fearlessly bled and died that that honor might be maintained."

Warming to her theme, she continued, "And now they will soon be returning. To what? Does any reasonable person imagine to the old order of things? To submit to being strung up, riddled with bullets, burned at the stake? No! A thousand times no! . . . They will come back to face like men whatever is in store for them and like men defend themselves, their families, and their homes."

Her fury spent for the moment, Walker closed her remarks in a somewhat milder tone. "Please understand," she told Schieffelin, "that this does not mean that I wish to encourage in any way a conflict between the two races. . . . My message to my people is this: Go live and conduct yourself so that you will be above the reproach of anyone—but should but one prejudiced, irrational boast infringe upon [your] rights as men—resent the insult like men."

During the first few months of 1919, Walker stayed close to home, writing political letters, hosting occasional dinner parties, and enjoying Villa Lewaro. Then, in late April, her friend Jessie Robinson, one of the first Walker agents and the wife of newspaper publisher C. K. Robinson, asked her to come to St. Louis to help launch the new line of Walker products. Although Walker was suffering from a severe cold, she decided to make the trip.

On Easter Day, a few days after she arrived in St. Louis, Walker became seriously ill. Alarmed, the Robinsons arranged for their doctor and his nurse to accompany their friend back to New York. At Walker's request, the St. Louis couple chartered a private railroad car on the era's fastest train, the 20th Century Limited. Other passengers, according to Walker's secretary, Violet Reynolds, expressed great curiosity about their fellow traveler, this mysterious "'colored woman' whose room was filled with flowers."

As the train sped across Ohio and Pennsylvania, Walker talked about all her still-unfinished business: She intended to build a girls' school in Africa, to construct a new office building and factory, and to put up a housing development for the poor in Indianapolis. She also wanted to take a European vacation that summer.

Arriving in Irvington weak but still determined, Walker got down to business at once, ordering her accountants to donate $5,000 to the NAACP's antilynching fund. News of the gift, announced a few days later at the NAACP's Anti-Lynching Conference at Manhattan's Carnegie Hall, brought a standing ovation from the 2,500 delegates. Walker's contribution, the largest the organization had ever received, so moved the convention that one wealthy black farmer from Arkansas pledged another $1,000 on the spot. Supporters, each of them expressing hope for Walker's recovery—"God spare you to the race and humanity," said a typical message—pledged $3,400 more within a week.

But Colonel Ward held out little hope for his patient. The effect of her high blood pressure, he said, had hopelessly damaged her kidneys. After she heard Ward's diagnosis, Walker sat by the fireplace in her bedroom, pulling her heavy, cream-colored silk shawl tighter around her shoulders. Then she summoned Ransom.

When the attorney arrived, Walker gave him a list of groups she wanted to help. "Madam Walker gave $25,000 to colored organizations and institutions," reported the *New York Age*. "Intimate friends believe she fully realizes the seriousness of her condition and wanted to do what she could for deserving race institutions before passing away."

One morning, Walker managed a faint smile as her secretary read her the latest letter from A'Lelia, who was traveling through Central America on a sales trip with Mae. Eliciting the smile was A'Lelia's news: She had decided to marry Ward's protégé, Dr. James Arthur Kennedy, who had just returned from Europe with the croix de guerre.

A few days later, Walker's nurse heard her say, "I want to live to help my race." Then she slipped into a coma. On the following Sunday morning, the *Chicago Defender* would later report, the day "dawned bright and warm. Outside, where the trees and lawn were green and pretty, the flowers blooming and the birds merrily singing, all was gaiety and happiness.

"Inside, where several people gathered around a beautiful four-posted bed and watched a magnificent soul go into eternity, all was grief and sorrow." Breaking the silence, the paper continued, Dr. Ward "turned to those around the bedside and said, 'It is over.'" Sarah Breedlove Walker, 51 years old, died on May 25, 1919.

Notified of her mother's death, A'Lelia rushed home from Panama. Meanwhile, 1,000 mourners attended funeral services at the Villa Lewaro, which concluded with a reading of Walker's favorite Bible passage, the 23rd Psalm. "Farewell, farewell, a long farewell," said the minister. When A'Lelia and Mae arrived, they joined a circle of close friends and accompanied Walker's rose-covered casket to Woodlawn cemetery, where it was buried after a brief graveside ceremony.

Tributes began to pour in at once. Walker's friend Mary McLeod Bethune called Walker's life "an unusual one." It was, said Bethune, "the clearest demonstration, I know, of Negro woman's ability recorded in history. She has gone, but her work still lives and shall live as an inspiration to not only her race but to the world."

Among the countless grieving admirers was journalist and author George Samuel Schuyler. Writing in *The Messenger*, he said, "What a boon it was for one of their own race to stand upon the pinnacle and exhort the womanhood of her race to come forth [and] lift up their heads." Walker, he added, "had given dignified employment to thousands of women who would otherwise have had to make their living in domestic service."

W. E. B. Du Bois, who wrote an obituary for *The Crisis*, said, "It is given to few persons to transform a people in a generation. Yet this was done by the late Madam C. J. Walker. . . . [She] made and deserved a fortune and gave much of it away generously."

Indeed, Walker's concern for those in need became even clearer after her death. Her will named A'Lelia as her principal heir, then listed dozens of organizations and individuals as beneficiaries. She

Wearing one of her trademark jeweled turbans, A'Lelia Walker Robinson strikes a jaunty pose in 1925. After her mother's death, A'Lelia became something of a Harlem legend, famous for her flamboyant style and lavish, celebrity-studded gatherings. Like her mother, she died in middle age, suffering a fatal stroke at the age of 46 in 1931.

Walker's business outlasted its founder by several decades: Here, Walker Beauty School graduates and officials—including Walker's friend and 1919 hostess, Jessie Robinson (seated third from right)—assemble in St. Louis in the 1930s.

established a $100,000 trust fund, its proceeds to go to "worthy charities," and left sums ranging from $2,000 to $5,000 to such institutions as the Colored Orphans' Home in St. Louis, the Home for Aged and Infirm Colored People in Pittsburgh, the Haines Institute in Georgia, the NAACP, and Tuskegee Institute.

America's first black, self-made female millionaire, Walker never forgot her roots. A child of poverty, she eagerly shared her immense wealth with the needy. Deprived of an early education, she made a point of supporting schools. Born to former slaves, she vigorously exercised her rights as an American citizen, using her economic and personal power to strengthen her community and urging others to follow her lead.

Walker's success sprang from her innovative line of beauty products and techniques. But the Walker

Method involved more than cosmetics: It taught black women to develop their natural beauty, thus improving their self-esteem and enhancing their confidence.

The Walker company employed thousands of people, both during its founder's lifetime and for decades afterward. Today, countless black Americans can name a relative—an aunt, a grandmother, perhaps an uncle—who served as a Walker agent. Walker's products enabled these women and men to educate their children, build homes, and start other businesses.

By recounting her own story, Walker encouraged black women and men to pursue their dreams. "I promoted myself," she often told her audiences. "I had to make my own living and my own opportunity! But I made it! Don't sit down and wait for the opportunities to come. Get up and make them!"

A woman of extraordinary courage and vision, Walker paved the way for the generations that followed her. The grit and determination that carried her from a cotton field to a mansion, from penniless obscurity to riches and national recognition, continue to inspire Americans who yearn to realize their own possibilities. ◖◗

CHRONOLOGY

1867	Born Sarah Breedlove on December 23 in Delta, Louisiana
1874	Orphaned when both parents die in yellow fever epidemic
1878	Moves to Vicksburg, Mississippi, with sister, Louvenia
1882	Marries Moses McWilliams
1885	Gives birth to daughter, Lelia
1887	Widowed when McWilliams dies; moves to St. Louis with daughter
1905	Moves to Denver and develops formula for Wonderful Hair Grower
1906	Marries Charles Joseph Walker and changes name to Madam C. J. Walker
1908	Moves to Pittsburgh and opens Lelia College
1910	Moves to Indianapolis and builds factory
1912	Travels throughout United States selling products and speaking to major black organizations; donates $1,000 to Indianapolis's black YMCA; divorces C. J. Walker; becomes grandmother when daughter adopts Mae Bryant
1913	Travels to Caribbean and Central America on sales trip
1916	Moves to Harlem in New York City
1917	Convenes first annual Madam C. J. Walker Hair Culturists Union of America Convention; visits President Woodrow Wilson, urging him to make lynching a federal crime
1918	Completes and moves into Villa Lewaro, a Hudson River mansion; becomes millionaire as Walker company annual sales exceed $250,000
1919	Contributes large sums to NAACP antilynching fund and other causes; dies on May 25 at Villa Lewaro

FURTHER READING

Barnett, Ida B. Wells. *Crusade for Justice.* Chicago: University Chicago Press, 1970.

Bird, Caroline. *Enterprising Women.* New York: Norton, 1976.

Gatewood, William, Jr. *Slave and Freeman: The Autobiography of George L. Knox.* Lexington: University of Kentucky Press, 1979.

Giddings, Paula. *When and Where I Enter.* New York: Morrow, 1984.

Hine, Darlene Clark. *When the Truth Is Told: I. History of Black Women's Culture and Community in Indiana 1875–1950.* Indianapolis: National Council of Negro Women, 1981.

Huggins, Nathan. *The Harlem Renaissance.* London: Oxford University Press, 1971.

Jones, Jacqueline. *Labor of Love, Labor of Sorrow.* New York: Basic Books, 1985.

Lewis, David Levering. *When Harlem Was in Vogue.* New York: Knopf, 1981.

Logan, Rayford W., and Michael Winston. *Dictionary of American Negro Biography.* New York: Norton, 1982.

Painter, Nell Irvin. *Exodusters.* New York: Knopf, 1977.

Sterling, Dorothy, ed. *We Are Your Sisters: Black Women in the Nineteenth Century.* New York and London: Norton, 1984.

INDEX

PICTURE CREDITS

———— ❦ ————

A'LELIA PERRY BUNDLES is the great-great-granddaughter of Madam C. J. Walker. Currently a producer with ABC News's "World News Tonight" in Washington, D.C., she was educated at Harvard and Radcliffe Colleges and Columbia University Graduate School of Journalism. Bundles, who lives in Alexandria, Virginia, frequently gives speeches about Madam Walker.

NATHAN IRVIN HUGGINS is W.E.B. Du Bois Professor of History and Director of the W.E.B. Du Bois Institute for Afro-American Research at Harvard University. He previously taught at Columbia University. Professor Huggins is the author of numerous books, including *Black Odyssey: The Afro-American Ordeal in Slavery*, *The Harlem Renaissance*, and *Slave and Citizen: The Life of Frederick Douglass*.